The Essential Gaudí

Jordi Bonet i Armengol

The Essential

Gaudí

The geometric modulation of the Church of the Sagrada Família

English translation by Mark Burry

Pòrtic

This work was awarded the
Institute of Catalan Studies 1999
Lluís Domènec i Montaner Prize
for Architectural Theory and Criticism

With the suport of

DESIGN AND LAYOUT
Domènec Òrrit

PHOTOGRAPHS ©
Salvador Redó, Jordi Bonet, Jordi Faulí,
Church of the Sagrada Família archives Joaquim Camp,
TAVISA and ECSA

DRAWINGS
Josep Gómez, Jordi Coll, Juan Carlos Melero, architects
(Polytechnic University of Catalonia)
Àlex Vila (Technical Office, Church of the Sagrada Família)
Mark Burry, architect (formerly, Victoria University of
Wellington, New Zealand, now, Deakin University, Australia)

Second edition:
october 2001

Exclusive publishing rights:
ECSA
Diputació, 250 - 08007 Barcelona
www.editorial-portic.com
portic@grec.com

PRINTED BY
IG Ferré Olsina, SA
Viladomat, 158-160 - Barcelona

ISBN: 84-7306-729-0
Legal deposit: B.29.724-2001

Acknowledgements

Without the example and the esteem my father, Lluís Bonet i Garí, always held for Antoni Gaudí i Cornet, I do not believe that I would ever have felt the interest in Gaudí's work and in the study of his theories I have had since my youth. My thanks for his teachings and those of the architects who preceeded me in the direction of the work on the Church of the Sagrada Família. I should also like to thank the architects Joan Margarit and Carles Buixadé, in charge of structural calculations for fifteen years, along with Josep Gómez Serrano, who worked, in co-operation with Jordi Coll, on the computer-assisted drawing made at the Polytechnic University of Catalonia Vallès School of Architecture. Thanks, too, to Jordi Faulí, on-site assistant architect and always ready to find solutions for problems with drawings or photographic reproductions, with the excellent assistance of Àlex Vila. I am also endebted to Mark Burry, who translated the original Catalan text into English with the same interest he brought to bear in making the computer an effective tool for speeding up our work, to the team at Enciclopèdia Catalana, who undertook publication of the book, and to Domènec Òrrit, who designed it. My gratitude goes out, too, to the jury who awarded my work the Institut d'Estudis Catalans' Domènech i Montaner Prize, and to Fundació Caixa de Sabadell and Fundació Enciclopèdia Catalana, whose assistance made the publication of this book possible.

Finally, a special thank-you to all those anonymous workers, from the foreman down to the stonemasons, bricklayers, model-makers, etc, whose efforts are helping to make Gaudí's dream a reality.
Laus Deo.

J. B.

Summary

Gaudí the man

The Catalan architect Antoni Gaudí i Cornet (1852–1926), son of a copper-smith from Reus, graduated from the Barcelona School of Architecture in 1878. Due to the humble economic position of his family, he helped defray the costs of his studies by working for a number of Barcelona architects and developers. From his youth onwards, his cultural and social concerns led him to form part of the Renaixença movement, which vindicated the identity of his country of birth, Catalonia and through such cultural institutions he came into contact with many Catalan intellectuals. The confidence shown in him by Eusebi Güell i Bacigalupi, one of the most important industrialists of his time, was such that Güell became Gaudí's patron, appointing him as his architect.

Gaudí's friendship with the ecclesiastical community in Reus led to him being commissioned to build the Archbishop's palace in Astorga and the Teresian School in Barcelona. At the same time he continued to gain professional stature, leading other Barcelona industrialists and magnates to commission him with the design of buildings in the expanding Eixample district of the city: Casa Calvet, Casa Batlló and Casa Milà. Blessed with a remarkable gift of

Colònia Güell crypt.

observation, he developed a personal architecture based on applying what he learnt from nature to his work. The knowledge and experience he acquired over the years was further enriched thanks to the various commissions he received from Güell. From the Palau Güell to the Parc Güell and the Chapel of Santa Coloma de Cervelló –Colònia Güell– these works were all important experiences which Gaudí would later apply in the work on the Church of the Sagrada Família, which he directed until his death.

An exceptional commission

Towards the end of 1883, Gaudí received the commission to take over the construction of the Church of the Sagrada Família. Considering this the most important opportunity an architect could wish for, he made it his life's work, devoting more than forty years exclusively to working on the project. Now in his prime, Gaudí dedicated practically one-third of his professional life to the undertaking. Though his brief was to continue the work commenced by Villar, he quickly won the confidence of the Association of Devotees of Saint Joseph, which was promoting the building of the church.

The Altar of Saint Joseph was wholly designed by Gaudí and was finished in 1885, whilst the crypt was roofed by 1891. It is said that the founder of the Sagrada Família, Josep Maria Bocabella, had dreamt that an architect with blue eyes would build the church, and he and Gaudí, who indeed had blue eyes, quickly reached a full understanding which, along with a generous anonymous donation, allowed Gaudí to undertake a completely new design. The result was Gaudí's great project, into which he threw himself with all his creative power with the intention of building his church.

Gaudí at sixty

In 1912, when the construction of Gaudí's Casa Milà —his last major secular project— was complete, he continued working for Count Güell on the chapel of the Colònia Güell and Parc Güell as well as, needless to say, the Sagrada Família and Majorca Cathedral, but little else. He had not yet resolved his conflicts with the city authorities, which arose from his construction of La Pedrera (Casa Milà) according to specifications exceeding the regulations of the time.

Gaudí had reached the age of sixty, quite an advanced age for that time and, despite the fact that he was not generally in the best of health, he remained, broadly speaking, in excellent condition. His daily habits included rising early and showering in cold water all the year round before walking uphill towards Sant Joan de Gràcia, where he took mass prior to making an early start at the Sagrada Família works. A frugal breakfast allowed him to keep up with the rhythm of construction, attend to the illustrious visitors who would turn up from time to time, lunch and continue his research work beside his collaborators. He would finally set out for the Ciutat Vella district of the city in the early evening, where he would pray before the Holy Sacrament in the Church of Sant Felip Neri before finally returning to his house in Parc Güell to rest.

Friends and admirers

This austere, simple healthy lifestyle did not prevent him from keeping up-to-date with events in the city, nor from staying in touch with his friends, many of whom were prominent personalities in Catalan life. The poet Joan Maragall had died not long before, in late-1911. Maragall's articles had become an important vehicle of support for the construction of the Sagrada Família Church, and he even portrayed the building as the most emblematic of monuments of the Barcelona of the future in the verses of his "Oda nova a Barcelona" (New Ode to Barcelona) which the great poet had written shortly after the terrible events of the 'Tragic Week' in July 1909. Gaudí maintained a respectful and friendly relationship with Dr Torras i Bages, and was an admirer of Enric Prat de la Riba, Lluís Millet and of the Orfeó Català choir.

These personalities valued the work of Gaudí highly, particularly as regards the construction of the Sagrada Família Church. After Gaudí had spent some time with Dr Schweitzer, later to win the Nobel Prize, Schweitzer noted in

Gaudí with Bishop Reig and Prat de la Riba. Photograph published in December 1914.

his memoirs how impressed he had been by the architect's intellect, comparing him to Ramon Llull. Most of Gaudí's colleagues and students who visited him and heard him speak also had the highest opinion of the Catalan architect. Clearly, too, new currents of opinion were also being formed which were to become severe in their criticism of Gaudí.

Life at Parc Güell

From his house in Parc Güell, Gaudí must have looked down on the growing city as the belltowers of his church rose ever higher. Gaudí had shared a simple family life in the house in Parc Güell with his father, who died in 1906, and his niece, Rosa Egea. They were assisted by the Carmelite nuns of Saint Joseph, provided through the good offices of the founder, Mother Rosa Ojeda. Mother Montserrat Rius, who had just entered the community at that time as a young girl from the village of Santa Creu in La Segarra region, is still alive at the time of writing. The help she gave Gaudí in his last years in his house in the Guinardó district of Barcelona included cleaning the house, washing and ironing and preparing the frugal meals he ate.

Count Güell also spent time in his house in the park, later converted into a school. Perhaps the architect and his patron discussed the unaccountably poor outcome of the project for this garden city, an idea practically no one seemed capable of understanding. Only three houses finally resulted from the considerable economic and promotional efforts of Eusebi Güell and the planning and architectural endeavours of Gaudí himself, who had devoted his creative energy to offering exceptional living conditions in this well-placed, sunny area of Barcelona. With the eloquent name of 'La Salut' (health), the lower area of the site, between Sant Josep de la Muntanya and what is now Plaça de Santllehy, was like a great coomb or valley in the flank of the mountain, overlooking the growing city and the sea.

Gaudí accompanying a group of visitors to the Parc Güell.

Gaudí's solitude

With the death of his niece in 1912, Gaudí was left alone in the house at Parc Güell. In 1914, the death of Bishop Campins and misunderstandings with the canons of Majorca Cathedral led to Gaudí leaving the project unfinished. Francesc Berenguer whom Gaudí called his 'right hand', also died in 1914. Despite these misfortunes, he drew encouragement from groups of enthusiastic architecture students who visited him regularly. He also received a visit from Enric Prat de la Riba, President of the Catalan Mancomunitat, accompanied by doctor Reig, Bishop of Barcelona, who came to see the work at the end of the same year. However, the general economic crisis also affected progress and jeopardised the continuation of the work. Besides selling his properties in Reus, Gaudí took to asking for alms, whilst campaigns in favour of the work were also launched. Various group visits were made to the church, including that led by the president of the Catalan Association of Architects, Bonaventura Bassegoda i Amigó, whose colleagues also made donations, and one from the Catalan Ramblers' Association in February 1917.

Monuments to Josep Torras i Bages and Enric Prat de la Riba

The deaths of Bishop Torras i Bages, the friend with whom Gaudí had founded the Sant Lluc Art Circle, on 7 February 1916, Prat de la Riba on 1 August 1917 and, finally, his patron, Eusebi Güell i Bacigalupi, on 8 July 1918, must surely have affected him profoundly. For the first two, Gaudí left, in the shape of the most extraordinary models, sketches for memorial monuments.

He proposed that the monument to Torras i Bages be placed beside the Passion Façade of the Sagrada Família, which he had left as a legacy and challenge to be taken up by his followers. This was a beautiful vertical composition in plan and elevation. It was characterised by new forms, a confluence of his research and geometrical studies inspired by nature, the essence of what he had planned for the nave and aisles of the church.

The design for the monument to Prat de la Riba took the form of vigorous pencil sketches which he presented to one of his young admirers, the architect Lluís Bonet i Garí, a frequent visitor who had just taken his degree. As the Town Architect of Castellterçol, he was commissioned by the local authority to design a square and a monument dedicated to its illustrious son, the wise governor of Catalonia.

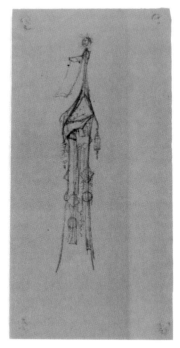

Sketch by Gaudí for the
monument to Prat de la
Riba (1918).

The house in Parc Güell that
served as Gaudí's home from
1902-25 and which now
contains the museum.

The Essential Gaudí

The Essential Gaudí

The master's final years

Personal letter from Gaudí to Bishop Torras i Bages enquiring after the health of Eusebi Güell.

Sketch by Gaudí for the monument to Bishop Torras i Bages (1917).

Complete dedication to the Sagrada Família

Gaudí could see that nothing less than his complete dedication to his church would allow him to pass on all he had dreamed of, all that he carried inside, in full detail to his successors to enable them to continue the work with as many of the elements he had planned as might be, and with the greatest faith to the spirit of this new architecture, to which only he could give precise shape and form. He must leave perfectly-defined models with clear, precise geometric line and proportion.

> "His friend Maragall had died, followed shortly afterwards by his beloved patron Count Güell and the good doctor Torras i Bages, Gaudí became submerged in the most complete solitude. 'My greatest friends are dead; I have no family, no clients, no wealth, nothing. I am therefore able to dedicate myself completely to the church.'" (1)

Gaudí was aware that work of such proportions could not be completed by his own generation. He often spoke of those who would be his successors and, despite leaving them the chance to use their own creative skills, he was convinced that his project, with its new architecture, needed to be expressed, as far as possible, within certain parameters, a certain geometry. This is to say that the project needed to be completed in accordance with a discipline of exact science so that it could take shape in complete faith with his thinking.

The Essential Gaudí

Summarised description

The construction of the Church of the Sagrada Família had begun in 1882, promoted by the Association of Devotees of Saint Joseph, founded by Josep Maria Bocabella, in accordance with a Gothic Revival project drawn up by the diocesan architect Francesc de P. Villar. Gaudí was commissioned with the direction of the work shortly after Villar's resignation.

Since the beginning, work on the church has depended exclusively on donations from the faithful. A particularly generous contribution allowed Gaudí to take the project onto a new, more ambitious plane, one in accordance with the vision he held and had written about regarding the significance of a Christian church.

The great complexity and the many years required to build an important church led Gaudí to propose the construction of a façade —the Nativity Façade— which would testify to the contribution of his own generation. Thus, taking as his starting-point the crypt which Villar had begun to build, Gaudí drew up the project for a church with a Latin cross plan with a nave and two aisles in the transept and crossing and nave and four aisles leading up to the main front. There were to be three main façades, each crowned by four bell

Original drawing by Gaudí of the Sagrada Família project.

"The dream realised" drawn by Joan Rubió –one of Gaudí's collaborators– published in the La Veu de Catalunya in 1902.

towers. These are the Nativity Façade facing east, the Passion Façade facing west and the Glory Façade facing south. Over the crossing, the great dome representing Jesus Christ, crowned by a cross of four arms 170 m high. Four smaller cupolas flanking this great dome represent the four Evangelists. Another cupola crowning the apse is dedicated to Mary, Mother of God. To date, only eight of the eighteen towers planned have been completed. The overall interior dimensions of the Church are as follows: 90 m long by 60 m in the transept and 45 m in the aisles. The columns which support the ceiling vaults represent local churches whilst the apostolic churches are represented by the crossing supports. Those of Catalunya around them, with those of other

Catalan-speaking regions. In the nave, those of the archdioceses of Spain and in the aisles, those of the five continents. The vaults and ambulatory are 30 m high, the nave 45 m high, the cross 60 m high and the apse 75 m high.

A cloister surrounds the whole church, separating it from its surroundings. Two buildings or sacristies are situated at either end of Carrer Provença, whilst the chapels of the Baptism and of the Eucharist occupy either end of Carrer Mallorca.

In terms of structure, Gaudí planned the church to be extraordinarily light thanks to the inclined columns which branch out symmetrically, following the lines of force to produce the synthesis of geometrical forms and structure which characterises his new architecture.

Drawing of the church project by Lluís Bonet i Garí.

The star-shaped square

In 1915 the first edition of an album was published describing the Sagrada Família as it was and as it would be. The album explained the programme for the works, showing what had already been done and what the church would later become through drawings and plaster models.

It was no longer what was described in *La Veu de Catalunya* in 1906 as "the dream come true", nor what was presented at the 1910 Paris Exhibition, including a 1:25 scale model of the whole of the Nativity Façade to which the novice architect Josep Maria Jujol had added colour. Nor was it only the drawings of the overall site which was offered to the city, what was contained in the six silhouettes corresponding to the vertical elevations of the planned Plaça Estrellada, or star-shaped square, which Gaudí proposed to Barcelona City Council. This inspired and daring solution was a response to the proposal the Council had made to Gaudí as to how the surroundings of the church currently being built could be resolved within the parameters of the Jaussely

The Essential Gaudí

Overall view of the church

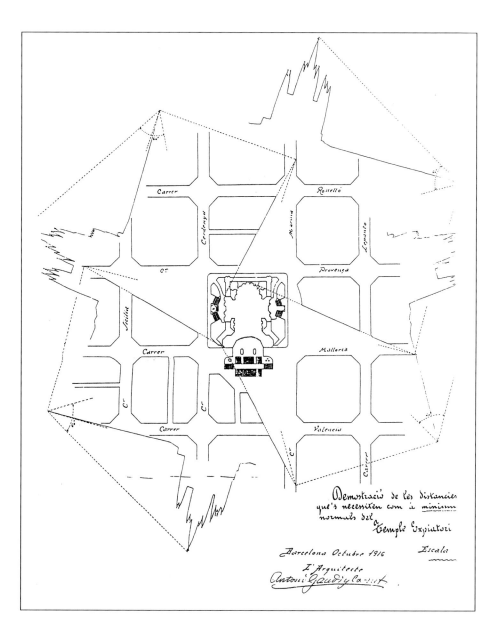

The surviving plan of the star-shaped square signed by Gaudí in November 1916 and conserved in the city archives. The plan demonstrates the minimum distances required for a normal view of the church.

Plan. This was something of an exception to Gaudí's general relations with the city administration. Unfortunately, the proposal was not accepted.

The architect proposed a solution for the church surroundings which took into account the economic difficulties of a local authority which could not devote large resources to the expropriation of building land within the Eixample district of the city but which, nevertheless, appreciated the monumental aspects of the church with an optimal sight-line set at thirty degrees. It was, without doubt, Gaudí's vision of the completed Sagrada Família Church, with an unmistakable silhouette which would serve to identify the city of Barcelona, between the sea and Montjuïc, above the plane and right in the centre, to the Collserola hills. It was perhaps from this star-shaped square, which will now never be possible, that the idea emerged for opening up Avinguda Gaudí. Despite their larger surface area, it cannot be said of Plaça de Gaudí and Plaça de la Sagrada Família, which open up to the east and west of the church respectively, that they embody the solution Gaudí proposed.

The plans for the church surrounds which Gaudí presented for the approval of the municipal project in 1916 were recently discovered in the city archives. The solution put forward contains no trace of the one Gaudí had proposed years earlier. It was greatly diminished in scope, showing that neither the politicians nor the technicians understood what Gaudí was suggesting. For this reason, Gaudí continued to insist on his solution, demonstrating, moreover, that by adopting it more than one thousand square meters of expropriated land would have been saved. The silhouettes of the completed church are mutilated by the authorities' solution. The star-shaped square allowed two façades always to be seen at the same time at the optimum vertical and horizontal viewing angle of 30 degrees. These plans were published in 1928 in Ràfols i Folguera's book *Gaudí*, yet the city council had no knowledge of the existence of the proposal for such a volumetric and urbanistic site which Gaudí had officially presented.

Drawing by Gaudí published in the Propagador de la Devoción a San José and comprising the first study of the church from the apse. The initial Gothic revival solution continued to be improved whilst remaining unchanged with regard to the symbolism of the general church layout.

The Essential Gaudí

Verticality

Despite all, what is important is precisely what these silhouettes created, the precise overall vision that Gaudí dreamed of, for volume and verticality of his building. This vision is gradually built up from the general plans, forming a light, balanced structure growing out of a Latin cross plan with three great façades, vaults and roof supported by inclined columns which branch out as they reach up from the crossing to a truly remarkable height. Gaudí went rather further than this schema, to a plastic art inspired by his observation that nature exploits the straight line, used to generate the various light, strong, warped surfaces combined one with another, in a starred microuniverse in which simple proportions are repeated, multiplying and forming a new architectural creation never previously imagined, complex yet simple, facilitating the path of those who would in the future inevitably have to continue and complete the work of this genius.

Everything is providential

Gaudí was perfectly aware that he would not be able to bring the great church to completion in his lifetime. He was, however, convinced that the future would provide, firstly, the support of future generations who would continue the work already begun; and, secondly, what experience had already taught him in the highs and lows of the long years of his involvement with the work of the Sagrada Família. He was often heard to say "with the Sagrada Família everything is a matter of providence".

His very appointment as the architect for the work was a chance affair, as it had already been commenced by the diocesan architect Villar and by a group, the Association of Devotees of Saint Joseph, known as the Josefins, founded by

Exhibition of the models
up until July 1936.

Inverted photograph of the hanging model with which Gaudí planned and calculated the Colònia Güell church.

Josep Maria Bocabella and with whom Gaudí had previously had no contact at all, but with whom he identified. This was, above all, due to his contribution both in terms of architecture and spirituality which had led them to evolve little by little.

But he needed to leave a clear definition of what he wished the church to be. The details he himself gave were not enough, nor the flame that he ignited within the other collaborators. It was necessary to specify certain forms precisely, to define exactly that which his successors would have to do, not so much in an absolute and definitive manner, but with sufficient elements to allow the work to be continued in the same spirit and, above all, with a clear idea of the structure and shape formed by his vision of space and colour.

Lack of other work allowed him to devote himself exclusively to the Church up to the end of his life. There were almost fifteen years of tenacious research, the results of which were committed not only to paper but as 1:10 scale gypsum plaster models which could be understood by those wishing to follow in the master's footsteps and whose own efforts would be rewarded by the results achieved.

Domènec Sugrañes, Architect Director 1926-1936 and Francesc de P. Quintana, Architect Director 1939-1966.

Isidre Puig Boada and Lluís Bonet Garí, directors of architecture between 1966 and 1983.

The continuators of the church

Gaudí also left the door open to the future creativity of those who followed him. He himself admitted: "I am seventy years old, and with what remains of my life, I will not be able to do all that the church requires." (2) Regarding the continuation of the church he commented:

"It is a cause of pain to me that I will not able to finish the church. I am growing old and it will fall on others to become renewed (…) providence will provide for the future direction of the church for, after all, everything about the Sagrada Família is a matter of providence." (3)

He added that the spirit of the monument should always be conserved, but that its existence must depend on generations which will transmit life to it and with which it lives and takes shape. (4)

Gaudí went on to state that:

> "I know that the personal taste of the architects who follow me will influence the work, but this does not grieve me. I believe that it will even benefit the church. It will mark changing times within the unity of the overall plan." (5)

With the certainty that he must work ceaselessly in order to make his ideas as clear as possible, but also that his successors should be able to understand and assimilate the architecture he planned, Gaudí intuited that the church would continue to rise as long as popular support was forthcoming, that is to say, as long as providence continued to manifest itself.

Nature as a model:
the 1:10 and 1:25 scale models

In his construction of La Pedrera house, Gaudí had expressed his creativity through the use of volumes and forms from lines so completely free as to appear simply the result of intuition, whereas we can be quite sure that they are a well-considered expression of the inspiration he received from nature.

Gaudí wished to apply to architecture the forms that nature suggested to him and in which there is no discontinuity. It was necessary, however, to suggest them volumetrically. A drawing over a plan was not enough. Geometry therefore became the way by which Gaudí could transmit to his successors that which, without it, would have been impossible to follow. Considerable personal

Final photograph of the
Sagrada Família Church
models (1922-1926).
The model for the sacristy
is located at the base.

dedication was required to achieve this, and the cost was also high, as each element had to be the stone reproduction, metre by metre, of what had first been formed in gypsum plaster. Thus he carried out his final studies using 1:10 scale models of all his geometrical forms. These, as well as clearly resolving the design of the nave and aisles with details studied in depth, were the clear formulation of the new architecture Gaudí wished to apply.

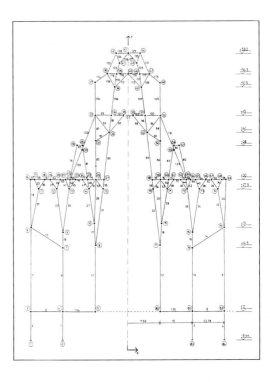

Structural scheme for the nave by Margarit and Buixadé.

But he went even further, for example determining for each high window the sculptures that should adorn it, representing the fruit, leaves and harvesting of a given plant, placed according to their order of appearance in nature. This begins with medlars, followed by cherries, apricots, etc, finishing with oranges, chestnuts and pomegranates. He even left resolved issues such as where to place the reflectors which were to illuminate the glass in the windows, as well as determining how the light bulbs would have to be changed. Once each of the details of each window, column, junction and ceiling vault, had been studied at a scale of 1:10, Gaudí would make a 1:25 scale model, gradually building up the entire site, adding all the repetitive elements, used to explain the work to visitors to the church. These models were on show in the crypt beneath the eastern façade (Saint Barnabas), as can be seen in various photographs.

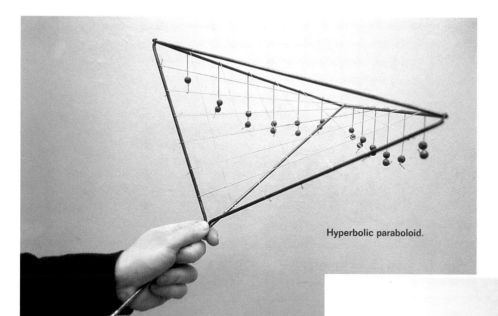

Hyperbolic paraboloid.

Mathematical model with which Gaudí studied ruled surfaces and their intersections.

Hyperboloid of revolution.

Structure

In 1923, Domènec Sugrañes gave an important lecture to the Associació d'Arquitectes de Catalunya (6). In it he described the system of calculation and construction techniques that Gaudí wished to use to build the Sagrada Família Church.

Whilst up until the end of the century Gaudí had been improving on the Gothic Revival style of his predecessor Villar and had raised the ogives, the experience of the Colònia Güell chapel proved to him the feasibility of inclined columns and the distribution of loads through a tree-like system, translated into a reticular spatial structure, one which transmitted the forces directly down the thrust lines.

In reality, the discovery of the surfaces of helicoids, hyperbolic paraboloids and hyperboloids of revolution impelled him to use them with all their potential in the church. Gaudí saw the helicoids as representing movement and

The Essential Gaudí

the hyperboloids of revolution light. Structurally, they were synthesised in the tetrahedron that he called the synthesis of space. (7) Thus Gaudí's structural conception can be summarised as the use of spatially reticulated, that is to say, spatially triangulated, structures. Just as the triangle is non-deformable in plan, so is the tetrahedron in space.

The two systems of bunches of generatrices form a hyperboloid of revolution from the straight lines that glide around a circular or elliptical path following an asymptotic inclination, one system clockwise, the other vice versa. Each set intersects on the surface such that two adjacent generatrices in each direction form triangles. This is similar to the hyperbolic paraboloids based on spatial quadrilaterals. These also form non-deformable structures through the two systems of generatrices of hyperboloic paraboloids that compensate when subjected to forces of tension. This is an entire structural system based on geometrical forms generated from straight lines.

Geometry

Gaudí's mastery of space and profound knowledge and experience of construction were complemented by his powerful, exact geometrical clairvoyance. Just as in rationalism then, vertical and horizontal planes form the basic structural system with all the difficulties that derive from them. Through the double curvature surfaces also generated by straight lines (hyperbolic paraboloids, hyperboloids of revolution, helicoids), it is possible to form non-deformable reticulated structures in space which lighten and simplify the assembly. These straight lines which form them as they generate them allow a series of star shaped forms to be obtained which combine some surfaces with others, coupling direct or inverted hyperboloids as open or closed forms, massive or empty, over which light glides and sounds are transmitted. Moreover, they disperse their loads, following their lines of force towards the base, forming a complex arrangement of elements which, without breaking the continuity, lighten the structure, providing new solutions which are harmonious, geometrical and rational.

Unfortunately, all the drawings and notes that Gaudí left at his death, well looked after in his studio, were destroyed, and all that remained were the gypsum plaster and models, even these broken into pieces. Happily, through patience and hard work and the in-depth studies carried out by the architects and technicians who had worked with Gaudí, the models were rebuilt, though little more could be done given the scant resources available. These were subsequently drawn. This was a vital task as it provided the basic elements for a deeper understanding and study of the Gaudí's ideas.

Studies focused on construction

It is some sixty or seventy years since Gaudí left us the reasonably well-structured description of his new architecture, expressed in photographs, published plans and the gypsum plaster models which are the admiration of one and all. Only the need to approach the construction process, the business of moving from 1:10 scale to full-size, made it necessary to find out what each element was. Until then, it had been possible to reconstruct the model Gaudí had worked on over the final years of this creative undertaking from the existing moulds and models.

What was missing was the knowledge of how Gaudí had come this far and, above all, on what he had based his approach. Certain parameters and proportions or a modulation did exist. Now, through the use of computers, all this has become much more simple. It has become relatively easy to describe each

Restored plaster models of the vaults which had been partially destroyed during the Civil War (1936-39).

The Essential Gaudí

element and each surface, to determine how to obtain starred intersections, since the computer can find the solution which both makes it possible for a single point to be common to various intersected surfaces and give the plasticity of expression which Gaudí sought.

Gaudí's last period

In 1921, when Gaudí was close to his seventieth birthday, he decided to make a whole bay, down to the smallest detail. Whilst until this moment the workshop had contained the solutions for the structure and the plasticity of the nave's composition, along with those which Gaudí had studied, but which he had found unsatisfactory over the course of the years, it was now a case of finding the definitive solution, that being applied for the Nativity Façade bell towers, up to a height of 100 m, with the colourful Venetian mosaic and the geometrical forms full of symbolism and possibilities that can be found on the finials to the towers.

This is Gaudí's last achievement, that is to say, the result of his final creations. Of them only the photographs and the reconstructions of the 1:10 models are known. Some of the elements Gaudí built up in his workshop and which are revealed to us now in the course of the research into them are required in order to continue the building in line with the master's conception. This facilitates knowledge of Gaudí's new architecture and, looking to the future, will be useful for completing that which he was not able to finish himself.

At the same time, whilst technique and research bring us closer to this objective, it is also true that only the intuitive refinement of the people would allow the work to be continued thanks to their donations. Without the anonymous, disinterested support of hundreds of thousands of the faithful, the miracle of raising the church would not have been possible, nor could it be continued in the absence of an answer to the question as to when the building will be finished.

Finial to the bell tower dedicated to the apostle Saint Barnabas, which Gaudí was able to see free of scaffolding on November 30 1925. This shows the form, colour and symbolism: the essentials of his new architecture.

The Essential Gaudí

Location of the studio

The workshop studio where Gaudí and the model makers made the 1:10 scale models stood beside what is referred to today as the Church Technical Office, more precisely the different buildings now occupied by the rectory and the parish offices on the corner of Carrer de Provença and Carrer de Sardenya. The larger part of the studio contained the 1:10 scale model used to study the church nave and aisles, as well as the tubular bells. There were also the plaster models for the Nativity Façade sculptures and a structural study. Gaudí gradually replaced parts of the model with others which improved the partial solutions he planned. Over the last few months of his life, he converted a small space near his work table into a bedroom. Josep Gómez Serrano's book *L'Obrador de Gaudí* provides a detailed description of the building.

Surviving fragments of the original model confirming Gaudí's intentions regarding the returns for the crossing clerestory windows.

Gaudí's research work

Gaudí's research work required both time and peace, both of which he had due to the slow progress of construction, a consequence of the shortage of financial resources. As the sculptor Matamala explains regarding the study of the models, Gaudí reserved the study of the models as his own research work, adding that he lost all sense of time when he was making them with the model makers. Months, even years would go by before each piece was ready. (8)

For example, to make the model for a column he had first to draw it, then form the sections which corresponded to each completed gyration, that is to say, corresponding to 8, 16, 32 and 64 flutes in the case of the 8-sided columns. Then the model maker had to "braid" the flutes, passing from one section to the next while the setting plaster was still pliable, with the aid of a ruler. Fortunately, there still exist some original examples that demonstrate the work required. Something similar was also true for the final solutions for the column capitals or 'knots', based on macles between the ellipsoids. Just to draw one of these capitals or 'knots' faithfully now took the best part of a year of painstaking work —though he was not exclusively devoted to this task the whole time— by the technical architect Antoni Caminal.

Gaudí invested considerable dedication in reaching these definitive solutions. Intermediate stages can be divined from the photographs of his study and from the sections of the 1:10 model used to develop the design. The nave columns, for example, form a volume which amorphously links the intersection of the column below with the five which form the branches of the tree canopy structure, passing through a number of circular elements used in an attempt to resolve this difficult point tried to the definitive solutions using the macle of ellipsoids, allowing the formation of the nave column knots or capitals. These are different from those of the crossing and the apse, despite the fact that they all emerge from the same ellipsoids.

Gaudí's desk in his study-workshop at the Sagrada Família site.

Gaudí was a master of his art, and intervened personally in a variety of matters, from making lamps to drawing sketches for sculptures, but always had collaborators to help him develop his ideas, so different and which, after reflection, needed to be put into effect and tested. His own enthusiasm enabled him to communicate what he was thinking and to motivate others. Needless to say, his collaborators were familiar with the task that they were working on directly, but they did not have a clear idea of the process as a whole. The best informed person was Gaudí's assistant architect and successor Domènec Sugrañes, whilst Francesc Quintana was familiar with the creative process behind the making of the columns as well as the structure of the central cupola, as it was he who had drawn it. It was probably not he, however, who developed the 'knots' (column articulations), formed from macles of ellipsoids, or other details. It is natural, therefore, that Quintana was not able to explain them.

The Essential Gaudí

In order to be able to write his book on the church (9), published in 1929, Puig Boada examined Gaudí's files and archives. He even held on to part of this documentation until just a few months before the fire and destruction that took place in July 1936. How he regretted not having kept the material for a little longer!

Thanks to these studies we have an idea, above all, of Gaudí's general ideas and, particularly, the symbolism and iconography Gaudí planned. We do not know, however, about his creative and experimental processes, details of which may have been discernible from his sketches and notes. His immediate successors may have had enough to go on with the definitive versions of the original 1:25 and 1:10 scale models, which they considered eloquent enough and which, thanks to their extraordinary commitment and loyalty, they were able to rebuild.

Structural design

Original model of the 'knot' or capital for the nave columns composed of ellipsoids.

By 1898, the structural design for the whole church had been completed (10), correcting all the defects Gaudí pointed out in the Gothic. By raising the height of the arches, the forces were made more vertical and the arches resembled parabolas with a peak of 2.5 times the light in the bay. This structural arrangement was completely superseded by the final arboreal solution that Gaudí continued to develop based on his earlier experience with the Colònia Güell chapel. This was an equilibrated arbiform solution with inclined columns branching out, following the thrust lines determined by the vertical loading, achieving an

Structural study: a comparison of the Sagrada Família Church with the cathedrals of Cologne, St Peter's in Rome and St Mark's in Venice. Published in *Àlbum* in 1925.

overall assembly of extraordinary lightness. Gaudí explained: "The dead loads need to be divided up and, consequently, the number of active components increased." (11) It was not until the last decade of his life, however, that the new architecture he brought to the undertaking was finally resolved. It is for this reason that he commented: "I am satisfied with the last model of the church nave and aisles, but I am sorry that I shall not see even one bay completed." (12)

This is consistent with another significant comment Gaudí made after many years of work:

"I don't believe in improvisation in the slightest –nothing is ever improvised– nor do I believe that inspiration can reduce my work, rather that it should be granted as something extra." (13)

Once the general structure was established, it was necessary to determine precisely the forms which would give it plastic expression. In truth, Gaudí resolved the spatial enclosure by using a web of tetrahedrons which formed a stiff, articulated assembly through helicoidally based tree-like columns and the use of ceiling vaults made from open and closed hyperboloids of revolution. In the assembly, each element worked both in support and in being supported. Furthermore, through the multiplication of many elements, the actual execution of the work becomes simpler, as they are repeated. It is thus possible to provide grandiosity whilst dividing the forces to which the structure is subject. It is like making molecular or arboreal structure a reality in construcion, or, in the case of the columns, the right and left twisted formation of DNA cells, which are the explanation of the origin of life.

The straight line is indisputably the living organism that is combined and which is present everywhere. The straight line is the generator of both convex and concave surfaces, with which the great architect was able to offer, through complete devotion to his work, the new architecture of his church and which furnishes a vast range of possibilities for the future.

Destruction

The fire and accompanying destruction of Gaudí's studio and much of the church itself occurred just after the military uprising of July 1936. The schools also burnt down, and vaults and walls collapsed. After burning down the rectory, the fire passed into the studio and workshop, full of papers and highly flammable materials. Once the roof with its timber beams collapsed, nothing could survive the flames except the incombustible plaster models, and even these were broken into pieces. Having set fire to the crypt, the mob decided also to dynamite the towers. A civil guard and member of the Esquerra Republicana de Catalunya political party prevented this by pointing out that the bridge joining the two groups of towers could be put to good use as a machine gun post to repel a possible attack by the fascists. (14)

Graphic representation of the destruction of Gaudí's studio, which was the site of all his drawing for his entire oeuvre, devoured by revolutionary fire in July 1936.

Salvage

Soon after these events, the architect Bonet i Garí, who had been appointed by Ventura Gassol, Generalitat of Catalonia Minister of Culture, as 'Collaborating Architect for the Salvaging of Artistic Heritage', managed to get a team from city services to collect the fragments of plaster models. These were walled up within the crypt of the church in the part that had been used previously to display the 1:25 and 1:10 scale models. The city architect, Josep Maria Martino Arroyo, responded promptly to this appeal for assistance. It was necessary on two occasions to reinforce arrangements for their protection.

Once the war was over, the reconstruction of the crypt commenced, along with the first reconnaissance and classification of the model fragments, directed by the architect Francesc de P. Quintana, as Gaudí's successor, Domènec Sugrañes, had died in 1938. His sons describe how the destruction of Gaudí's studio had sunk this courageous man's morale, because he was sure that the fire and subsequent disappearance of all the plans made any continuation of the work impossible. His sadness and pessimism about any possible revival of his country precipitated his death.

Restoration

At the suggestion of Bertran i Güell, just before the Civil War started, the Construction Committee had deposited in a London bank one million pesetas from the funds set aside for continuing the work and, particularly, for the construction of the sacristy, as had been agreed in 1936. This money was enough to restore practically all that remained of the crypt. It was therefore made possible to recommence religious services, leaving everything much as it had been and as it continues to be now. It is good to know that there were still

Patient restoration work and subsequent investigation.

Restored original model of
the lateral nave window.

craftspeople, as well as the head of construction himself, named Brasó, who had worked with Gaudí, and that, although they were not made directly by Gaudí, there are timber assemblies such as doors and furniture, and liturgical decoration conserved which can be considered original elements.

The exacting task of restoring Gaudí's models was an undertaking the architects Isidre Puig Boada, Lluís Bonet i Garí, with Francesc de P. Quintana, very soon took up and to which they devoted themselves wholeheartedly. From 1941 onwards, architecture students used to come to draw plans of particularly exceptional elements. It was necessary to take the measurements of the pieces in order to find their position in three dimensions and in this way to ascertain the geometry of the intersections of the warped surfaces. In the crypt beneath the Nativity Façade, where the models had been exhibited, the modellers' workshop was set up under the direction of Pere Sunyer. All the fragments, large and small, were identified and classified little by little, and reconstructions were made of the best-conserved elements and those of which photographs existed or plans had been published. Jordi Brunet continued the work until 1960, when Jordi Cusó took over. The work was partially sponsored by Felip

Detail of the 1:10 scaled original model for the vaults of the side aisle.

Bertran i Güell, grandson of the first Count Güell who, with his cousin, Eusebi Güell i Jover, maintained the family presence on the Construction Committee. Quintana, who had been directly involved with drawing the columns, defining their measurements and, particularly, Isidre Puig Boada, who had published his book on the church in 1929 (15) and had made in-depth studies of the plans and models to ensure that his text was as well-documented as possible, were decisive in this work.

Fortunately, many moulds of the vaults and the columns existed due to the repetition of the elements. For this reason, it was soon possible, what with the surviving positive and negative casts, as well as the symmetries, to make exact restorations of each model at both 1:10 and 1:25 scale.

The Essential Gaudí

The Essential Gaudí

Gaudí's studio and the continuation of the work

Original 1:10 scale
fragments of the
arches, which match
the geometric models.

Window, pediment and
finial for the side aisle
façade, now restored.

All the most important elements of the volumetric studies for the Glory Façade survive, and it will be possible to arrange these in good faith in due course. Naturally, the original models for elements Gaudí never got round to considering do not exist, such as solutions for the cupolas crowning the apse and the crossing, although the principal lines are known from surviving drawings and, particularly, the process by which Gaudí intended to realise them, based on his experience of the construction of the sacristies. Quintana explained that he had drawn the principal cupola over the crossing from a prone position on the ground, as the scale at which he was working obliged him to use wrapping paper and a drawing board would have been too small. Gaudí used a simpler model to calculate the structure for the Sagrada Família than for the Colònia Güell chapel, avoiding the complexity of the latter.

This task has still not been completed, however. It is being done gradually, as necessary and as it becomes possible to deduce that an unknown fragment is exactly the one missing in a particular assembly.

As matters stand, the room in which hundreds of classified fragments from Gaudí's original models are stored is organised in such a way as to aid the reconstruction of all that is necessary to deepen understanding of Gaudí's studies and for all that will need to be built in the future.

The model-making workshop today, a continuation of that of Gaudí's time, where he undertook his investigations. This is where the original models are restored, moulds and other valuable items stored and full-size models made.

The Essential Gaudí

"Nature is my master"

Gaudí's capacity for observation is well known. He himself explained that this was a consequence of his weakness of health since childhood. The contemplation of nature, besides giving him pure pleasure, also helped him form ideas enabling him to reach such insights as "architecture *creates* the organism and that is why the latter must have a law in consonance with those of nature." (16) These ideas matured over time: "Everything comes from nature's great book." (17) "This tree next to my studio: that is my master." (18)

The Reus Manuscript already contains, however, in its in-depth study of the church, the germ to which he would add all that he gained from his experience of other projects and which he would later carry over to the Sagrada Família.

"I was able to test the structure for the Sagrada Família first at the Colònia Güell. Without this preliminary test I would never have dared to adopt it for the church." (19)

Side aisle vaults which support the columns and their branching.

It is not surprising, therefore, that he did not wish to complete a definitive project, despite the pressure to do so from Bishop Josep Morgades at the beginning of the century. He needed to confirm his ideas. His initial vision of verticality can be clearly seen in a drawing from 1890 showing three fronts, each with four bell towers and the spires over the crossing and apse. This is reaffirmed in the drawings of the complex published by his assistant Joan Rubió at the beginning of the century, and in which Gaudí himself drew and made changes to some of the elements, such as the sacristies. The slow progress of the building work allowed him to develop these ideas. For this reason the overall view of the complex itself remained practically unchanged after this well-known visionary drawing was made. This was even more firmly fixed as a result of the proposal he made to Jaussely in 1906-1907 and which he reaffirmed in 1916 in his reply to Barcelona City Council regarding the town planning arrangements he felt should be made. Gaudí's vision enabled him to clearly define the setting he wished to give the church in the context of the city environment. The arboreal structure and the ruled surfaces are the result of the lessons from nature. Discontinuity does not exist in nature, but, in contrast, it does in architecture. It is produced by the supporting vertical elements meeting the supported horizontal elements. Gaudí achieved continuity by the use of these surfaces.

> "The purpose of construction is to free us from the sun and the rain; it is in imitation of the tree, and is therefore a collector of sun and of rain. The imitation extends to the level of the elements, for the columns were first trees: after which we see how the capitals become adorned with leaves. This is one more justification for the structure of the Sagrada Família." [20]

He therefore carried out in-depth study of the structure, the columns, the vaults, and they are the results of this study. It comes as no surprise that Gaudí should claim that:

"My structural and aesthetic ideas have an 'indisputable' logic. The fact that they have not been applied before and that I should be the first to do so gave me great pause for thought. This is the only thing which might make me doubt. Notwithstanding this, I believe that, convinced of their perfection, it is my duty to apply them." (21)

From Gothic Revival to a new architecture

In fact, Gaudí was obliged, through the commission he had received and his own wish to respect the work planned by the architect Villar, to accept the Gothic Revival style as his own. Fortunately, however, he was able to transform it little by little into a new, personal architecture inspired by nature and in which everything is different. It is clear that the large donation made in around 1893 allowed him to draw up his plans in the way he considered most fit, with the complete confidence of the Construction Committee. Gradually, therefore, he changed everything, from the crypt to the pinnacles over the apse, from the Gothic Revival windows and the bays of the cloister of the Nativity portal to the whole façade.

The transition from the Gothic Revival forms found in the crypt with a pointed arch between the buttresses between each bay in the nave, subdivided by smaller elements closed with ogives, is well resolved in the elevations of the nave façades.

The window of the lower part of the side nave, beneath the choir, is in a wholly Gothic Revival style, but is completely denuded of the mouldings, replaced by compound forms of hyperboloids of revolution where the arches are circumferences. These interlace with hyperbolic paraboloids and star-like

Side aisle façade. As the façade rises one can see the transition from Gothic Revival to the new Gaudinian architecture.

formations to form a sculpted lacework. The light glides past, as Gaudí liked to say. There are no significant obstacles to the passage of light and shade, because the geometry of the ruled surfaces, always generated by straight lines, forming both convex and concave surfaces of delicate proportions, allows light to pass through harmoniously. Over 20 m up, over the level of the choir galleries, the Gothic tendency of the window begins to give way to an organic combination of circular hyperboloids of revolution with an elliptical one, the straight line generatrices interlacing with star-like forms, and four other smaller ones. In the nave, the entry of light is augmented by a succession of larger openings. Just a great central elliptical hyperboloid of revolution flanked lower down by two smaller circular openings. The spires crowning each window are stretched, elongated to acquire greater length, culminating in great baskets formed in the side aisle by paraboloids and in which fruit is contained, and with symbolic elements, bread and wine, in the final spire over the higher windows of the central nave.

Thus, little by little, as the Church rose, Gaudí transformed the initial Gothic Revival to the new forms he had created, as occurs with the spires and the terminals of the bell towers, to which he even gave colour in the form of Venetian mosaic. For the Nativity Façade he made this gradual transformation from the base to the top. But it is clear that all its sculptural ornamentation can reach a point at which this notion is lost. For the lower part, up to a significant level, the windows are Gothic Revival. But from here onwards the bell towers each acquire their own personality and form, the new Gaudinian architecture taking shape and rising up forcefully. The parabolic envelope, the structural ribs, the louvers –inclined planes that scatter sound from the tubular bells around the church grounds– and, it goes without saying, the finials, are all completely different. There is nothing it can be compared with. Between 1923 and 1924, he completed the final model for the bell towers, and on 30 November 1925, the first tower could be seen completed free from its scaffolding. This was the only part of the creation he had dreamed of that Gaudí lived to see as a complete expression of his new

The new architecture at a height of 100 metres; parabolic forms of the structural ribs, geometry and colour.

architecture. One single completed bell tower, rising up to a height of one hundred metres to declare the pioneering nature of his research, the entirely new architecture, in form and in colour, he had created, was only a first sample. Though this was the crowning moment of his work during his own lifetime, it was in reality only the first fruit of his final years of toil: Gaudí's final work.

The Essential Gaudí

The columns

"Two years have been spent working tirelessly, meticulously and at a cost of four thousand *duros* [20,000 pesetas] to arrive at a complete solution for the columns."(22)

Description, work and research

Gaudí devoted many years of hard work and research to create a new column. More than this, he produced a new order which superseded the classical orders: Doric, Ionic, Corinthian, Composite and Tuscan, and all the variants that had given shape to architecture over the centuries. He did so in order to obtain sustained and sustaining vertical supports such as pillars, pilasters and columns, and horizontal supports such as lintels, arches and vaults which at the same time support the structures which cover spaces and hold up the roof.

Gaudí also sought to create an element which, as he observed in nature, had the look and expressiveness exteriorising all the force of the support, capable of sustaining great loads, but also reflecting the helicoidal movement of growing trees, an unequivocal sign of life.

In the repertory of historic styles, the Salomonic column is one exponent of this movement, rising as it grows, but Gaudí felt that it did not fully achieve the desired effect. And it is hardly necessary to point out how many Salomonic columns have been used to support constructions of grandeur, fully successful compositions, over the centuries, from the Romanesque and Gothic periods to Bernini's exultant baroque. The Salomonic column, however, in its apparent upward movement, denotes a possibility, but also a certain fragility, the incapacity to sustain great loads.

Gaudí persisted in his search for something which could be considered impossible. The Parc Güell features various solutions with inclined and

Parc Güell: helicoidal
columns, starting point
of untiring research.

The Essential Gaudí

Salomonic columns, and he had also experimented with his ideas at the chapel in Colònia Güell. But it was at the Sagrada Família workshop that his efforts finally came up with the ultimate solution. Firstly, he tried to commence from a square section with a base rounded by parabolas, rising helicoidally with base and capital commencing and finishing the vertical element of support. This solution was placed to one side, however, whilst he doubtlessly continued maturing this new creation through his knowledge of geometry and vision of space and volume, rarely found together in human intelligence.

He made this discovery when he was seventy years old, towards the end of his life, when he had accumulated the experience of a keen observer and tireless worker. Gaudí continued to investigate, though not from a square but from star-shaped polygons, the hexagon and the octagon, which he rounded with concave and convex parabolas at the points or vertices of each inner and outer point of the star. The Salomonic column which could be obtained from this base with a unidirectional twist −twisting the helicoid to the right− gave him the idea of composing it with a second Salomonic column with the same base or section, twisting to the left. The surprising outcome resulted in a new geometrical figure, the intersection of two surfaces which, when cut, bring into being edges born just at the axis of the mid points of the sides of the star-shaped polygons. Thus, from a star of six or eight points emerges a new star-shaped form with twelve or sixteen points. If this movement was continued, new edges emerged, finally forming a circumference.

All these movements are ordered into a progressive multiplication of edges while at the same time the twists occur at an ever lower height. Setting the component cylinders at a height of one metre and with the use of templates, Gaudí made plaster models at a scale of 1:10, the swept surfaces of which are produced through a movement that twists determined by the number of sides to the component polygons. And for each column it is always the same polygon.

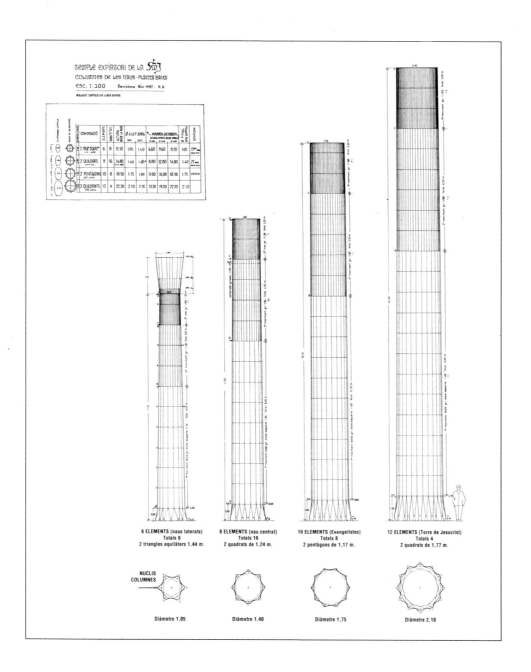

Gaudí's column; the surprising outcome of geometrical investigation. Drawing of plans and elevations.

The Essential Gaudí

Research into a new order

Drawing of the twelve-sided column supporting the crossing, and plaster model of the hexagonal base and the octagonal column realised.

For the starred polygon of six or eight points, the outcome is a twist of thirty and twenty-two and a half degrees respectively, rising helicoidally to a height in metres equal to the number of sides of the polygon. In this way, it goes from six to twelve and from eight to 16 sides. If a second twist is effected from the top of the first series using half the degree of rotation and to half the height, that is to say, from three and four metres, the result is 24 and 32 edges. To move on upwards by a quarter the number of sides to the polygon in metres, that is to say, by one and a half metres and two metres, the number of resulting edges rises to 48 and 64 respectively. If the process is continued still further the number of edges becomes infinite, giving a circular section at a point where the column reaches a height in metres double the number of sides in the polygon. Thus, for twelve and sixteen metre heights, the polygon becomes a cylinder and the total twist of sixty and forty-five degrees respectively, that is, the angle embraced by each side of the starred polygon. For the hexagon, sixty degrees is one sixth of the three hundred and sixty degrees of the circumference and for the octagon, forty-five degrees is an eighth part. Gaudí commented on the emergence of the new column with these words:

> "The stars follow the orbit which is the trajectory of their equilibrium; and what is more, they revolve, which is to say that their movement is helicoidal. The columns of the Sagrada Família follow an axis of forces which is the trajectory of their stability, which is their equilibrium; their generation is from a star-shaped section which turns as it rises; its own movement is, as such, also helicoidal (this also occurs in the case of tree trunks). The stars move and turn, as their orbits are closed lines; the column moves and turns because it has the movement of a double helicoid, the turn taking place in both senses."[23]

From in-depth study of the columns, it can be deduced that these twists conform to series:

The series to the elevations is as follows:

$H = n + n/2 + n/4 + n/8 + n/16 + n/32 + \ldots = 2n$, in which $H =$ high and $n =$ number of sides.

In the case of the octagon: $H = 8 + 4 + 2 + 1 + 0.5 + 0.25 + 0.125 \ldots = 16$ m.

In the same sense, the twists produced are:

$22°30´ + 11°15´ + 5°37.5´ + 2°49.5´ + 1°24´\ldots = 45° = 360°/8$.

Once Gaudí had the idea for this vertical geometrical form, just as he had been enthused earlier by the knowledge and the possibilities of the hyperbolic paraboloid and, later, by the discovery of the enormous plastic properties of hyperboloids of revolution, the combination of these helicoidal surfaces led him to continue studying them and to use them, one might almost say almost to play with them, with all the richness that they give to the light that touches them.

Thus he reconsidered the forms for all the structural elements for the division of forces with which he had given the church nave and aisles their equilibrium, combining all kinds of polygons with the diversity of columns, adapting them to the simple modulation from which they had been composed, as much at the base level of the church as in the longitudinal and transversal cross sections, and at heights of 15, 30, 45 and 60 metres, at each level, of the galleries, triforiums and ceiling vaults in the nave, aisles and crossing.

The image of the forest with its tree trunks, branches and foliage through which the light enters which Gaudí used to describe his idea of the nave and aisles gradually took shape through a modulated and ordered combination of major and minor columns. These ascended to be absorbed finally by hyperboloids of revolution. The roof vaults spring from the circumference which is the collar gathering the termination of the support element. In this way, Gaudí achieved the continuity he saw in nature.

View of side aisle vaults and columns, with the choir at the back.

The Essential Gaudí

The Essential Gaudí

Research into a new order

Series of columns.

Series	12	10	9	8	7	6	5	4	3	2	1
Inter-axis	90	75	67.5	60	52.5	45	37.5	30	22.5	15	7.5
Fractions	1	5/6	3.4	2/3	7/12	1/2	5/12	1/3	1/4	1/6	1/12
$\varnothing$	210	175	157.5	140	122.5	105	87.5	70	52.5	35	17.5

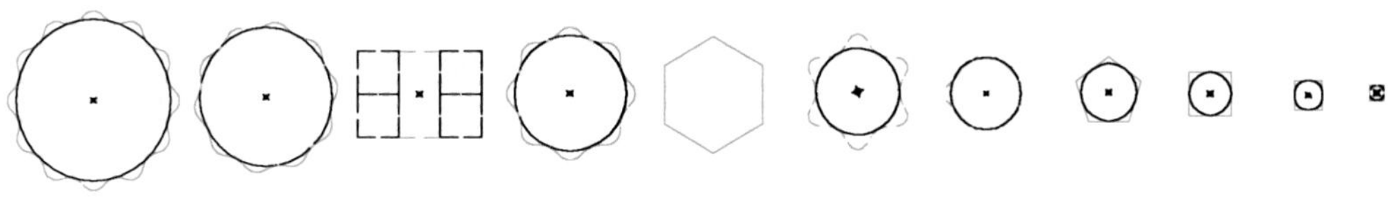

Nomenclature	Column 12	Column 10	Choir	Column 8	Evangelist	Column 6	Nave	Aisle		Cloister	

	210 -35=	175 -35=		140 -35=		105 -35=		70 -35=		35	
	6/6	5/6		4/6		3/6		2.6		1.6	

	3	2		2	1	2	2	1	1	1	
Hyperboloids $\varnothing$	180	150	135	120	105	90	75	60	45	30	15
Knot ellipsoid 8	360	300	270	240	210	180	150	120	90	60	30
Knot ellipsoid 10	450	375	337.5	300	262.5	225	187.5	150	112.5	75	37.5
Knot ellipsoid 12	540	450	405	360	315	270	225	180	135	90	45

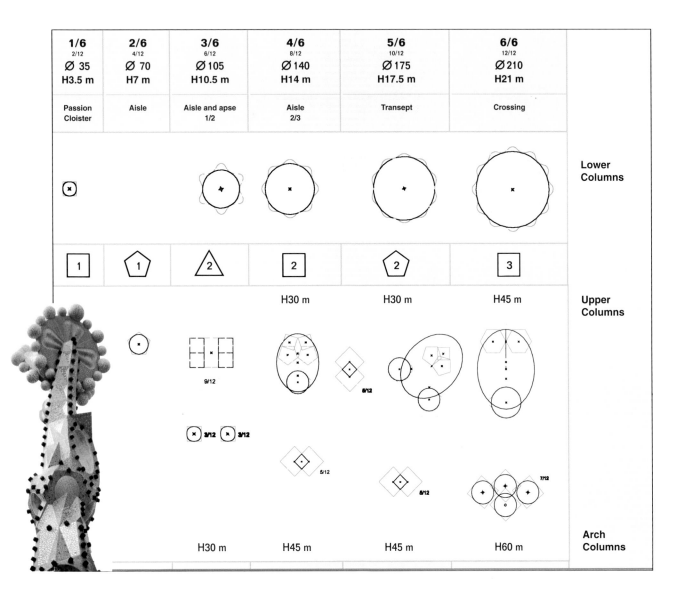

1/6	2/6	3/6	4/6	5/6	6/6	
2/12	4/12	6/12	8/12	10/12	12/12	
Ø 35	Ø 70	Ø 105	Ø 140	Ø 175	Ø 210	
H3.5 m	H7 m	H10.5 m	H14 m	H17.5 m	H21 m	
Passion Cloister	Aisle	Aisle and apse 1/2	Aisle 2/3	Transept	Crossing	
						Lower Columns
1	1	2	2	2	3	Upper Columns
		H30 m	H30 m		H45 m	
	9/12					
	3/12 3/12		6/12		7/12	
		5/12	6/12			Arch Columns
	H30 m	H45 m	H45 m		H60 m	

Original mould, conserved intact, allowing the reproduction of columns.

Research

Despite Quintana's oral transmission, the restoration of the models, and the construction in 1956 of the first column, which represented Barcelona and was made manually and with great difficulty, as it was necessary to cut them from stone and afterwards raise and build many columns, it was necessary to carry out in-depth study into how to make the drums from which the column is formed. The original models show a height of one metre. There exist important fragments of the six and eight-sided columns and above all an entire mould of the largest, at a scale of 1:10. After studying the exact elevations where the edges begin to appear, they were drawn to determine the exact geometrical generation before proceeding. A new model was made and compared with the one from the original mould. It was not possible to distinguish one from the other. In order to do the same for the other different columns, the conclusion was reached that they were the consequence of the same geometrical generation, which was repeated, along with the slenderness ratio, determined as being 1:10.

Gaudí planned the six sided columns which support the choir galleries to be made from Montjuïc sandstone, but the definitive model for the knot or capital did not exist, though the original sections had been drawn. In their place it was decided to reproduce the same form for the capital, albeit inverted, and generated through twists that were less separated in height, as if they had been compressed. This is a solution in accordance with Gaudí's own system. On seeing these columns, one is impelled to ask oneself how it would have been possible to divine the geometrical generation as conceived of by Gaudí without the direct transmission made by Puig Boada and Quintana in the former's 1929 publication and the latter's written explanations and numerical data for the diameters. This would have required a knowledge of geometry and a vision of space which could only be deduced with difficulty, no matter how much in-depth study and analysis this Gaudinian creation was subjected to.

From the central nave to the crossing, the following polygons appear:

Aisles	Nave	Transept	Crossing
hexagon	octagon	decagon	dodecagon
two triangles	two squares	two pentagons	three squares

The interior diameters of the lower columns (trunks) comprise a series based on the number 35:

105 +35 =	140 +35 =	175 +35=	210
Column 6	Column 8	Column 10	Column 12

The elevations up to the beginning of the knots or capitals and to the articulation where they rise as branches, that is to say, where the section becomes a circumference, are:

1/2	2/3	3/4	4/4
10.5 m	14 m	17.5 m	21 m
12 m	16 m	20 m	24 m

The slenderness ratio of the columns up to the knots is 1:10, and the bases are as high in units of ten centimetres as the number of sides for each polygon, that is:

6 sides 60 cm	=	6 dm
8 sides 80 cm	=	8 dm
10 sides 100 cm	=	10 dm
12 sides 120 cm	=	12 dm

This form of generation follows on at the different levels.

Nature and architecture.

The arboreal system

As has been noted, the arboreal system allowed Gaudí to use the same system to generate the columns —what can be called the branches— of the diverse support elements that rise up to the ceiling vaults. Use was made of various polygons as well as macles between them, though if necessary the entire number of twists could be omitted in order to adapt these columns to the different elevations. We can distinguish the support columns of the aisles from those of the central nave, transept and crossing, and the diversity and union between them at the different levels above the lower columns. When it suited his purpose, Gaudí inverted the sense of the column, so that the circular section is not always at the upper end. This made possible columns that multiply as they rise up, like the branches of a tree.

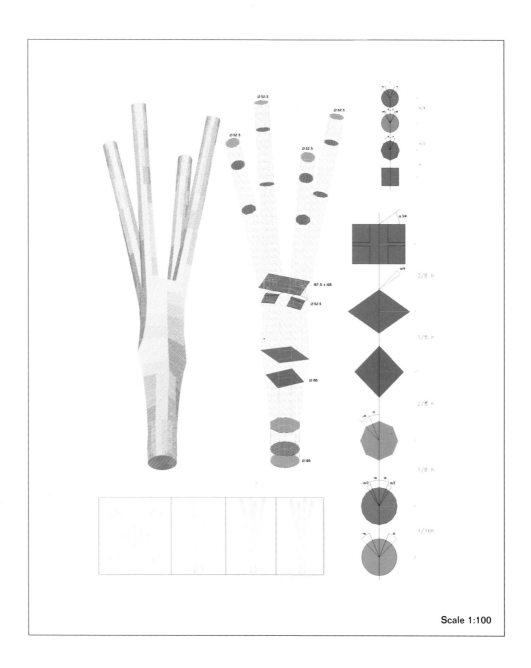

Column over the choir showing the ramification from one to four columns.
The upper columns are 52.5 cm in diameter, half that of the lower one which generates them.

Scale 1:100

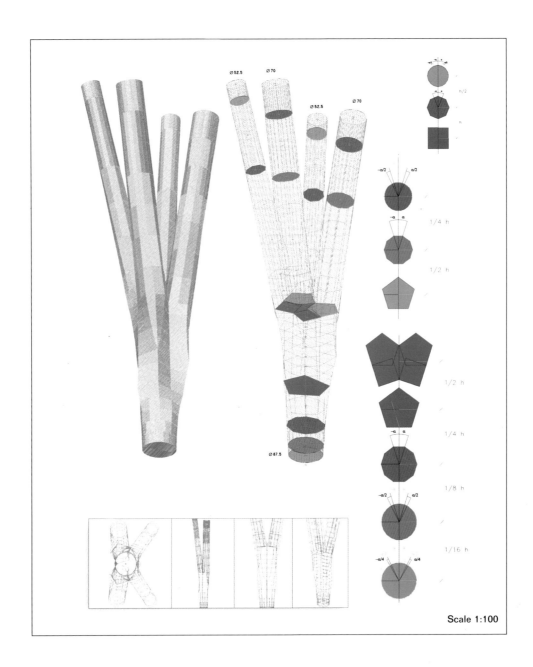

The same law of helicoidal generation allows progression from the macle of a pentagon and a square whose sides measure 52.5 cm to the lower circumference.

Scale 1:100

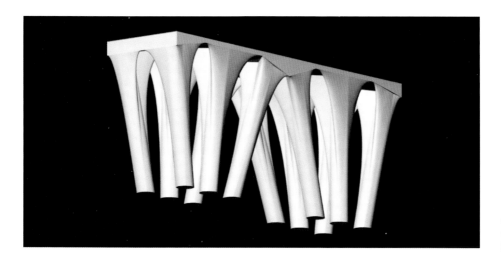

Columns supporting the nave window, generated by paraboloids.

Aisles and choir

Between 15 and 30 metres in height, the support consists of an inverted column, that is to say, that at the lower part and within the thickness of the choir a circular section is inserted which proceeds from a rectangle measuring 157.5 x 105 cm. This coincides with the inscribed diameter of the six-sided column supporting the choir. The twists convert it into a square at the first level, then to octagons, sixteen sides, etc, until the circular section.

Four equal columns with square bases with sides measuring 52.5 cm, that is, half of 105 cm, emerge from the upper part of the rectangle referred to previously. These, after appropriate transformation through twisting, connect with the collar of the hyperboloids of revolution that are the beginnings of the ceiling vaults. These columns are approximately 8 m high, although part of the lower end is grafted into the rectangular column. In this way a form of generation is accomplished which ties together the number of sides to each polygon (n) that generates the column –in this case 4– with the length in m (2n).

4 + 1/2	4 +1/4	4+1/8	4+1/16	4+...	= 8
2	1	0.5	0.25	+...	= 8
n + n/2	+ n/4	+ n/8	+ n/16	+...	= 2 n

View of the tree-like
columns, now built.

Side aisles and central nave

From the upper part of the knots or capitals for the central nave, between 15
and 30 m in high, a more important column emerges that rises, inclined to
provide support to the vaults that close the space at 45 m. There are two other
singular forms, which articulate as four supports, two by two. Of these, those
of smaller diameter pair up with those that stem from in front of the choir and
the other two, of greater sectional diameter, provide support for the vaults that
close at a height of 30 m.

These singular forms needed to be studied in order to understand their generation as, despite the faith with which they could have been passed from the
1:10 scale model to full-size, it did not seem reasonable to consider that Gaudí

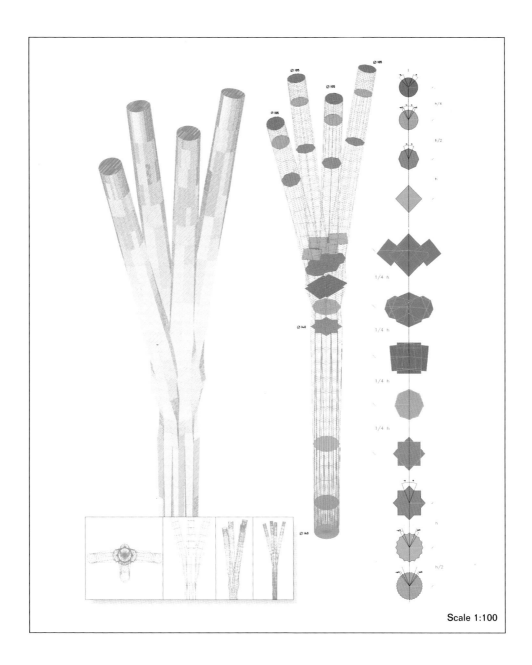

Scale 1:100

Through the application of the same law in the crossing, the lower circumference of 140 cm diameter, generated by two squares forming a star-shaped octagon, becomes four columns with a diameter of 105 cm supporting the vaults, ramified each one from a square.

Section through the
octagonal column.
It is based on an
eight-sided star whose
circumference is rounded
using parabolas.

would not have resorted to a geometrical solution. The most robust supports seem to have come from a pentagon, the two smaller ones from squares. The possibility of a macle of the two helicoidal forms needed to be considered. This was a solution that could not be discounted in the light of the presence of macles as geometrical forms on the finials to the bell towers. Thus, the starting-point was the coincidence on the same line of the macled 52.5 cm sides of a square and a pentagon, going through their corresponding twists.

The modellist J. Brunet invented a little machine to simplify the process of making the models at a scale of 1:10, derived from the base profiles, allowing the versions of the model to be compared with the original.

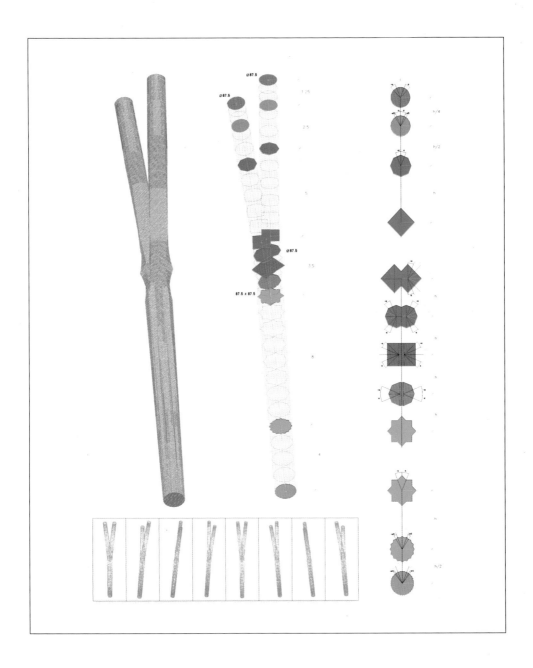

Bifurcation of the central nave upper columns. The octagon becomes both the lower circumference and the upper two columns, with the same generation law from the square to the upper circumference.

The Essential Gaudí

Research into a new order

The ramifications are produced with the help of knots or forms of transfer following the same law.

Upper central nave

The column for the central nave, 45 m in hight, is clearly derived from two squares without rounding the resultant star shaped polygon with parabolas as described previously for the 8 sided lower column of the central nave, although it is also inverted, that is to say that the lower end –that with the circular section– emerges from the knot. In this way, the two squares of the triforium elevation are able to generate the figure that transfers to the two columns. The upper support elements provide support which rise up to the highest vaults. This also gives the higher edges greater relief. The inscribed diameter and the side of the square both measure 90 cm.

Both the singular forms for the columns above the choir and the macle resulting from the knot formed by ellipsoids are truly surprising due to the resulting plasticity and the sense of domination over geometry which only such a master as Gaudí could achieve. The continuity of the uninterrupted line rising up suggests that the columns really do follow the thrust lines imposed on them.

Branching forms

This repetitive but singular generation is also seen in the forms of branching that bifurcate from one to two columns in the side aisles at a height of 30 m, corresponding to the triforium of the central nave and in which the different figures forming the transept and the crossing will be located, repeating the same method, though modified as required.

For the column at the end of the choir giving onto the transept, which may not have been studied by Gaudí, as there is no surviving photograph or model, the same system has been applied to obtain a support that possibly differs little from that which Gaudí would have planned. It is the result of fusing pentagons and squares through the use of inverted generation which passes first to a pentagon and which, other twists having been made, becomes a circle at the same level as the original, which emerges from the level of the choir.

The knots

'Knot' or capital of the central nave columns. The transition to a circle is hidden within the volume of the knot. The choir terraces and window can be seen lower down in the photograph.

Description, work and research

We call the various elements of transfer between columns, or of continuity between trunk and branches, 'knots' in accordance with the image of the wood and the trees that Gaudí liked to use to explain the nave and aisles of the church. Situated between the columns at different heights in the arboreal structure, they were not easy to obtain. For this reason, various solutions were applied to the 1:10 scale plaster model being built up in the workshop.

First there appeared the simple amorphous connection between the columns, followed by some surfaces like plates attempting to assume the function of reinforcing elements that would otherwise be little protected. Later on, and always in accordance with the lessons of nature, they appeared as stumps or knots without any geometrical definition and, finally, studies based on the fusion of ellipsoids offered up new solutions, despite being based on the modularity which, like an immense spider's web, extends throughout the church.

It must be added that Gaudí wished to make use of these elements to resolve the illumination of the nave. He therefore planned the use of ellipsoids which have hollowed-out concavities circumscribed by a necklace of hyperbolic paraboloids through which electric light can be indirectly reflected whilst, at the same time, through transparency, they decorate stained glass windows with the symbolism corresponding to each column.

There were two definitive solutions for these knots that Gaudí decided to employ according to the place and space at which they were located. For the twelve columns of the central nave and the transept, the most voluminous solution; for the eight columns surrounding the crossing, made from basalt

Restoration of the models at 1:10 scale.

stone, the simpler solution, more reduced despite being derived from the same ellipsoids. This same form also serves, in equivalent size, the eight-sided columns that surround and support the vaults of the apse and ambulatory. Finally, for the four great columns of the crossing, the first solution was adopted, appropriately proportioned.

Study

Once the time came to make these knots —those for which the reason, the origin and internal geometrical structure were unknown— from the original plaster models scaled at 1:10, it was necessary to take measurements with maximum precision of the principal, secondary and minor axes for each ellipsoid.

The opportunity to obtain diverse restored models, fortunately with a large proportion of what Gaudí himself had planned, allowed them to be measured in good faith. The result was surprising. Taking each measurement with absolute care, noted and on paper from the largest ellipsoid to the smallest, the measurements, in centimetres, were:

	major axis	secondary axis	minor axis	
	1	2/3	1/2	
Large ellipsoid	360	240	180	1
Medium ellipsoid	270	180	135	2/3
Small ellipsoid	180	120	90	1/2

The ellipsoids maintained the same proportions between their axes. If the larger could be regarded as the unit, the middle sized is two thirds of the largest, and the smallest, half.

Gaudí played with these elements in order to give them, in composition, a balance of volumes in relation to the columns that emerged above. Furthermore,

Basalt knot for the transept columns. The branching passes from the lower ten-sided polygon to the five columns above.

he was as likely to subtract part of the largest as he was to add. Moreover, he completed it with the decoration of the intradoses using star-shaped elements which were to enrich it like rays of light from some volumes, also ellipsoidal, which, with coloured stained-glass windows facing the exterior and the white light in the interior, could achieve a play of light of great quality as well as lighting the nave and aisles.

The study of these intersections of hyperbolic paraboloids, which grow and reduce in size as they join in a star-like configuration, was a long and exacting process. It probably took as much as a year's work to adjust them to axes and

The Essential Gaudí

Research into a new order

Porphyry column
supporting the crossing
with the commencement
of the pale granite 'knot'
or capital.

measurements –those of the original model– as we sought a method unknown to us.

Gaudí decided upon two distinct models for the knots, one with greater volume that corresponds to the transition of the 140 cm diameter granite columns. This had the major ellipsoid fused with others of smaller dimensions decorated with a necklace of hyperbolic paraboloids. Another, also originating from the same ellipsoid, but more reduced because the upper part was cut with the intersection of inclined planes and the lower part by trimming through the subtraction of part, cut out by a smaller ellipsoid. This second type allows for the close spaced columns in the apse. The intercolumniation of the nave is a more generous 7.50 m between axes, whereas this dimension reduces to half in the apse, at 3.75 m, requiring a less bulky solution. This second type is also used on each of the eight columns with ten sides surrounding the crossing that Gaudí planned to be made from basalt.

Upper part of the pale granite knot and the branching of columns for the central nave.

The first varietal with the largest proportions crowns the four great columns of the crossing, which measure 2.10 m in diameter. These were to be made from porphyry, which is the strongest naturally occurring stone in compression, to support the great loading from the major cupola above which, as the highest point of the church, represents Jesus Christ. It is also the most bulky varietal that incorporates the nave lighting. It is for this reason that a pale coloured granite has been selected to reflect light. The same type is used for the four beneath the crossing.

The ceiling vaults over the nave and aisles

Exhaustive studies

Until a definitive solution could be found, this was an assembly of forms arranged in star-like formation from various hyperboloids of revolution which were articulated by the use of hyperbolic paraboloids and planes as both positive and negative shapes. Gaudí expended much time and considerable effort. We recall once more what Gaudí said to Bergós after expressing his satisfaction at seeing the first bell tower completed: "I am satisfied with the last model of the nave and aisles, but I am disappointed not to be able to realise a complete bay." (24)

He stated to Bergós after also telling him of his satisfaction at having seen the first bell tower completed.

Once the idea had been established at the end of the century to make the church larger, the solution adapted for the vaults was in accord with the Gothic Revival scheme, canting the ogives to centre the resulting thrust lines. There are surviving photographs of this important model of the nave at a scale of 1:25.

Later on, the hyperbolic paraboloid became the protagonist: "Now you see, the hyperbolic paraboloid which everyone has studied and which everyone knows to be useless, will now be used for the Sagrada Família vaults…" recalls Puig Boada in a long conversation on the vaults and the excellence of this geometrical form, which Gaudí related to the Holy Trinity. The experience of the Colònia Güell chapel was what persuaded him to use them. In his book Gaudí i la Sagrada Família, Martinell provides a full account. It is, however, only when one delves more deeply into the study of ruled surfaces that the hyperboloid of revolution appears to him to be the most suitable form:

"The volume is made by ruled surfaces from infinite generatrices, embracing the whole of infinite space. These surfaces, the hyperbolic

Original mould (negative) for the model of the nave roof scaled at 1:25.

paraboloid, the hyperboloid of revolution, and the helicoid, all have the same atomic structure, that is, the tetrahedron, which can be seen in the three surfaces mentioned. The tetrahedron is the synthesis of space. The hyperbolic paraboloid represents light and the helicoid movement." (25)

From the circle which transforms the polygonal, square, pentagonal, hexagonal or octagonal bases of the columns, in the twists produced as they rise, the hyperboloids of revolution are born, beginning and forming the nave and aisle vaults. Gaudí divides the whole of the surfaces covering each bay of 45 x 7.5 m into parts differentiated by the supports. To each side of the axis of the central nave are ten smaller columns which spring like branches from the columns below, providing support from the floor level of the church.

The Essential Gaudí

These actual hyperboloids of revolution combine with others that are inverse, that is to say, that are open at the collar to allow light to enter. They are joined together with others by star-like forms based around the common points of intersection that are also the result of the same modulation. The hyperboloids of revolution are generated from a circular directrix which is the diameter of the collar, maintaining between them the proportions of the unit, the two thirds and the half, in other words, 120, 80, and 60 centimetre diameters. From the original models of the ceiling vaults and their intersections, the star-like forms leave space to inscribe some hyperbolic paraboloids which at the same time make space for a series of smaller hyperboloids of revolution twenty centimetres wide and which also act as light sources. Just as Gaudí explained: "Light enters during the day just as through the midst of the leaves of trees. At night the occuli will appear as stars in the sky."

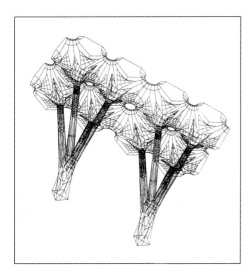

Side aisle vaults and columns (CAD drawing).

The side aisles and the choir

Gaudí left the star form complex for the thirty metre high vaults of the lateral nave clearly resolved. Between the windows at a height of between 15 and 20 metres runs the choir. These stepped terraces are the raised levels that run along both sides of the nave and aisles as well as the head, providing space for one thousand three hundred and fifty choristers to fill the church with their song during ceremonies. The choir ties the structure together and provides cohesion to the whole assembly. The undercroft is articulated by means of a combination of inclined hyperbolic paraboloids which join harmoniously with the upper parts of the windows and the six-sided columns. At their open horizontal edge there is a balcony made from a combination of hyperboloids of revolution that assists the overall lighting and provides support and decoration to the lower surface. The first bay was finished

Nave windows, walls
and columns.

by early 1993. It was the first time that the plastic effect, which Gaudí himself only ever saw in gypsum plaster ten times smaller, could be seen at full size. The impact of seeing the light gliding over the surfaces was surprising even to the many admirers of Gaudí's work, of which this was in any case but a first taste.

To raise the vault it was necessary, firstly, to put the columns in place, then construct the glass fibre moulds around them to make the vaults using reinforced concrete. Gaudí had often used such techniques previously. The little elevation of the hyperboloids was adequate for the system. The intersections of the various ruled surfaces were drawn by postgraduates at the Sant Cugat del Vallès School of Architecture, attached to the Polytechnic University of Catalonia, under the direction of Professor Josep Gómez Serrano, through a cooperation agreement signed with the Church Construction Committee, by which access was gained to the computer equipment needed for the work.

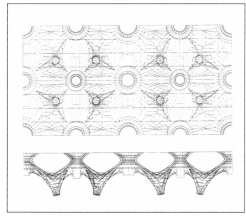

CAD drawing of the ceiling vaults (section and plan of the side aisle) a star form combination of ruled surfaces.

The hyperboloids of revolution in the aisles have collar diameters that range as follows: 60, 80 and 120 cm, which accords with the proportional system applied throughout. The smallest hyperboloid of revolution has a diameter of twenty centimetres. Planes complete the union between these and the surfaces of the windows where they meet on one side. On the other side there is a parapet formed from a decorated vertical hyperboloid of revolution with a collar measuring one 180 cm which completes the side aisle on the side of the central nave. This triforium follows the perimeter of the central nave around to the east and west transept façades where they meet then continue around the apse. As described in the lecture published in the annual proceedings of the Associació d´Arquitectes de Catalunya in 1923 (26), these vaults are now made from concrete modelled from polyester moulds and subsequent sprayed concrete using white cement.

The central nave and transept

The central nave, which rises to a height of 45 m, spans between windows supported at their lower parts by an extraordinarily beautiful assembly of inclined columns made from hyperbolic paraboloids. The upper part of the window here is a richer development of its equivalent in the side aisle. This is most apparent in the solution for the higher elliptical hyperboloid of revolution and the sculptural impact of the intersections between the hyperboloids of revolution on the interior face.

From side to side of the 15 m of light in the central nave, the eight sided column which springs from the knot –a fusion of ellipsoids– bifurcates into two branches ending in hyperboloids much higher than those in the side aisles. The hyperboloids of revolution in the vaults that align with the principal axes are of large proportions and intersect with each other forming stars that follow the generatrices that glide through the collars. In each bay there are five

Central nave vaults made using the Catalan vault technique. The generatices of the hyperboloids allow the introduction of symbolic palm fronds using Venetian glass.

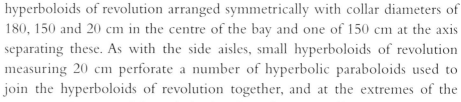

Detail of the central nave vaults. The divergence of the hyperboloid generatrices allow it to be decorated with Venetian mosaic.

Columns generated from paraboloids supporting the clerestory windows at a height of 30 metres.

Intersection of the lateral nave hyperboloids

hyperboloids of revolution arranged symmetrically with collar diameters of 180, 150 and 20 cm in the centre of the bay and one of 150 cm at the axis separating these. As with the side aisles, small hyperboloids of revolution measuring 20 cm perforate a number of hyperbolic paraboloids used to join the hyperboloids of revolution together, and at the extremes of the intersected hyperboloids of revolution small teeth made from hyperbolic paraboloids are used to highlight their interlacing.

These vaults could also be made using a traditional system of laminated tiles also discussed in the above-mentioned lecture, given that their magnitude makes them difficult to make using the glass fibre mould system. The generatrices of the hyperboloids are steel strips placed every 15 cm; these are supported by circular directices and allow ceramic tiles to be laid easily to form the intrados. The first leaf is made perfectly in the way Catalan vaults have always been built, by buttering all the edges of the tiles with rapid-hardening cement. The second leaf is then laid using Portland cement mortar, the tiles all cross-laid and aligned parallel to the circular directices of the hyperboloid of revolution. In order to gain the maximum benefit from the tiles, which measure 20 x 10 cm, especially where the space becomes more restricted, small pieces of Venetian glass are placed in the resulting gaps with the accompanying effect of enriching the ornamentation at the same time that the structure of the hyperboloid of revolution remains absolutely explicit. Gaudí wanted the central nave to be decorated with palm fronds –the palm symbolises the glory of martyrdom. The long thin triangular shapes thus formed between diverging adjacent rows of tiles following the generatrices provides an appropriate solution to this desired decoration using a combination of broken Venetian glass in various shades of green.

Details of the clerestory window and the hyperboloids of the central nave. Light glides over the surfaces just as Gaudí had anticipated.

The crossing

According to the architect Quintana, the calculation
and drawing for the
vaults over the cross-
ing had to be done
using large sheets
of wrapping paper
from a prone posi-
tion on the floor.
The fire destroyed
these studies, but
some of the numerical data and
original sketches remain, along
with elevations and sections of the
assembly published at various times.

Arches of the crossing
nave and transepts.
Distribution of the tiles
according to the directrices
of the hyperboloids.

Through an understanding of the geometry of
the nave and transept and the structural rationale
employed by Gaudí, it has been possible to
produce a 1:25 scale model from which all the
calculations for the vaults that cover the crossing
and the apse can be calculated.

The modules and proportions conform to the whole that Gaudí had wished
to give the church. The 210 centimetre diameter columns reach up to support
a further three that, as branches, support the evangelists' towers and that of the
central cupola. From 45 m up each of the four columns divides into another
four. The diameters pass to 140 and 105 cm and emerge from the three
squares for the 210 cm, to two squares for the 140 cm, and one square for the
105 cm. The proportions lie between the whole, two thirds, and a half.

The crossing covers 900 m² in a square with sides measuring 30 m. It is formed through the interlacing of 25 hyperboloids of revolution. There is one in the centre with a 4 m diameter, four at 3 m diameter situated on each axis. Between these are a further eight measuring 1.5 m, crowned by more of the same size but inclined. The centre has a diameter of twice two thirds of three, that is, 4 m. Between them is a formation of hyperbolic paraboloids perforated by smaller hyperboloids of revolution as seen with the nave and aisle vaults. The columns support them via massive hyperboloids of revolution in line with the stars that join the generatrices of these star-like vaults, a singular occurrence in Gaudí's architecture. Structurally, the tetrahedron –father of spatial geometry according to Gaudí– ties everything together to form a totally rigid assembly, thereby securing the stability of the 170 m high central cupola supported by the columns.

1:25 scale model of the crossing vaults.

It would be difficult to find a different solution to this, as it must link the form of the cupola that Gaudí wanted, which results from connecting hyperbolic paraboloid spindles to each other –as shown in the proposal for the vaults over the sacristies which provided with the experience of the structure and geometry. These forms, strong and at the same time light, well articulated as tetrahedrons, form a concrete structure which has to support twelve inclined columns which provide the rigidity to the terraced space planned for above the crossing ceiling vaults. Practically no other solution would be possible. The other four columns 4.50 m from the centre support the structure for the staircases and the lift towers which provide access to the highest point of the cupola, the cross, which is 170 m high.

View of the works facing
the apse (June 2001).

The apse

Gaudí planned to close the apse with a great hyperboloid of revolution
with a three and three quarter metre diameter collar open at the upper
extreme at a height of 75 m supported by twelve columns that surround the
presbytery and conform with the ambulatory which both joins and separates
the apse chapels. It is important to understand that Gaudí commented
repeatedly that on entering the church one should to be able to see the
whole of the interior as far as the apse and its decoration, unlike Saint Peter's
in Rome, whose excessively long central nave made it impossible to see the
end and, above all, had curtailed the view and grandiose proportions of the
cupola.

The published texts show Gaudí's symbolism, which situated the Pantocrator in the centre of the apse, made from Venetian glass mosaic with the angelic hierarchies of seraphims and cherubims, all illuminated by light which is to enter through the great oculus of the hyperboloid of revolution.

As stated previously, the crossing covers 900 m2 in a square with 30 x 30 metre sides. The axes join the hyperboloid of revolution through generatrices which generate a hyperbolic paraboloid serving as a transition. The support columns come from others made from granite and placed at 3.75 m one from another. They have the knots or capitals of least bulk, from which emerge branches: columns of different heights which, at the top, support the great apsidal hyperboloid of revolution which closes off at 75 m.

First computer drawing of the apse, based on Gaudí's drawings and his laws of geometry, structure and proportions.

The windows

Description

Gaudí projected three types of window, each progressively more different, as a means of ensuring a harmonious transition from the Gothic Revival to his own new architecture.

At the level of the underside of the choir, the composition is essentially Gothic Revival, but the mouldings have been replaced by new warped forms that allow the light to glide through for the side aisle windows above the choir up to a level of 30 m, the forms are clearly different. The principal element is an elliptical hyperboloid of revolution accompanied by four circular openings raised above a frieze of tall openings with a distinctive deep inclining windowsill. The exterior gable stretches upwards to a spire finial in the form of a basket made from hyperbolic paraboloids, which holds the corresponding fruit coloured by Venetian glass.

The third type of window, in the central nave, resembles the previous example, especially with regard to the central elliptical hyperboloid of revolution, but in this case it is flanked by two smaller, effectively circular, hyperboloids of revolution above the same four long openings which with the sloping sill complete the composition. The whole piece is supported by a triforium composed of an extraordinary composition of inclined columns more like balusters made entirely from hyperbolic paraboloids that wrap around the upper extreme of the side aisle vaults. Looking down the length of the triforium, the lower part of this window reminds one strongly of the corridors in Teresian schools. The elongated exterior pediment is also terminated in a spire like its lower neighbour, with a finial composed of the various surfaces that make up the roof. Letters forming the word 'Gloriam' occupy the rounded stars that go around the top of the major elliptical opening. The original 1:10 scale models of the terminals to the pediments survive. Gaudí wished to decorate them with Venetian glass: grapes and ears of corn, terminating them with the chalice and the Host.

Side aisle windows
dedicated to the
Founding Saints.

The Essential Gaudí

Study

Despite the fact that many original 1:10 models for all the windows have survived, rigorous study of the surviving elements has nevertheless been undertaken. There are also surviving drawings and excellent published photographs. For the lower sections, work was undertaken by the architects who had known Gaudí personally and who had recreated the drawings and subsequently built the first elements using artificial stone. For those over the choir, the New Zealand architect Professor Mark Burry began the analytical drawings in 1979-80, receiving a grant from the Construction Committee through the Càtedra Gaudí ("Gaudí Chair") in 1979-80, and went on to make the first studies using computers. This initiative allowed the adjustment between adjacent hyperboloids of revolution to correspond exactly with the original points, refining the coordinates of each point until all the hyperboloids of revolution made a faithful match with the original. Thus it was possible to find a solution that joined all the common points between hyperboloids of revolution which otherwise would only need to have the asymptote varied by a fraction of a degree for the result to be impossible to achieve. For the later study for the central nave the coordinates of each point were determined. The diameter of the elliptical and circular hyperboloids of revolution use the same proportions as the lower windows: the 1.5 x 3 m opening in the lower window is the equivalent of the 2 x 4 m opening for the upper window.

These windows continue around the transept and surround the crossing, a large square measuring 30 x 30 m. This solution comes across as the most coherent from the point of view of fluidity and structure, demanding precision and more massive structure for the returns at each of the angles between transept and nave or apse. The discovery of a fragment of Gaudí's original 1:25 scale model was very significant, as it has provided confirmation of the fidelity of the intuited solution. The combination of the rationalism of the structure, in complete concordance with the geometry that Gaudí planned, and the assurance that this discovery provides that Gaudí's intentions are sufficiently clear, mean

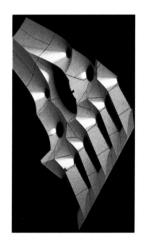

Computer drawing of the window volume.

Side aisle façade. The words 'incense' 'myrrh', and 'gold' (in Catalan) appear on the rainwater down pipe brackets.

Arches supporting the choir. Intersection of various paraboloids.

that his successors can follow them despite the fact that not all the original project has been passed down.

Part of the 1:25 scale mould for the upper part of this window was also found recently. This has also provided the confidence to complete what remains to be done. It must be said that Puig i Boada, Quintana and Bonet i Garí were able to reconstruct these models at a scale of 1:10, differentiating the parts which had been lost with an honesty and dignity consistent with the esteem and respect in which they held Gaudí's work.

The roofs

The first solutions

Gaudí also studied the nave and transept roof in great detail and wanted to have them built from slabs of Montjuïc stone. "The roof will be double and I want them both to be made from stone." (27)

There is part of the first solution made at a scale of 1:25 which was in sufficiently good condition for elements that make up the interior of the Nativity Façade to be started from the same model showing the roof bays of the Roser and Montserrat cloister. Some inclined planes have 4-5 cm thick slabs of Montjuïc stone laid in horizontal layers measuring 40 cm between joints and 25 cm wide. The quoin vaults in the Gothic Revival cloister provide them with support. The definitive solution fully differentiates the roof over the side aisle from that over the central nave and, of course, the domes.

Side aisle roof

This solution, replacing the earlier one, was demonstrated in the plaster models, and is formed from a combination of hyperbolic paraboloids which may possibly have resulted from comparison with the highly effective solution for the adjacent provisional school buildings.

In this manner, the side aisle roofs are covered with Montjuïc stone, which make a skin for the inclined elements and those below of double curvature, in order to let in as much light as possible enter through the central nave windows above the side aisles. The roof is composed of vaults made from brick laid on flat with the various hyperbolic paraboloids that conduct rainwater down towards the drainpipes arranged around the facade. Some pyramidal lanterns which support the prolongations of the columns above the level of 30 m with rhomboidal openings protected by some further hyperbolic paraboloids allow natural light to enter to the interior of the church through the collars of the hyperboloids of

Original photograph of the model of the nave roof, composed entirely of hyperbolic paraboloids.

revolution. Gaudí studied lamps that match the hyperbolic geometry, which could be hung concentrically within the collars allowing light to glide between the two facing surfaces simultaneously with the lower surfaces being covered in coloured glass tinting the light. The original 1:10 scale models for these elements, bearing symbols for Jesus, Mary and Joseph, are conserved.

Central nave and transept roofs

The roofs over the nave are a series of pyramids –bay by bay– merged into each other and the pediments to the windows below by large hyperbolic paraboloids. These are crowned by a series of aedicules decorated with symbols of the Holy Family. Each pyramid is crowned by a lamp tower reaching seventy metres in height. Reminiscent of the bell tower finials, they bear a vertical line of five shields that are inscribed iconographically with the letters "amen" and "al-le-lu-ia".

The space above the central nave and transept vaults is very high and is divided into several floors connected by spiral staircases. In each bay are four structural columns, continuations of those below. Three skylights protected by hyperbolic paraboloid canopies are arranged vertically up the pyramids to provide natural light to the interior. The inclined external surfaces will be covered with stone in a manner similar to that of the roof of La Pedrera.

The cupolas

The pyramidal assembly of the Sagrada Família is emphasised by the cupola crowned with a cross at 170 m representing Jesus Christ and situated over the crossing. It is flanked by four other cupolas, each 125 m high, representing the four evangelists. This group is flanked by a cupola over the apse crowned by a star symbolising Mary, Mother of God. In the drawing published in 1890 these elements were already in place, albeit in the Gothic Revival style. These combine with the twelve other towers representing the apostles, four for each façade, and together provide the distinctive character of the exterior.

Apart from leaving the bell towers of the Nativity Façade, Gaudí executed well-defined models for the Passion and Glory Façades and also gave the overall idea of the envelopes for the crossing and apse cupolas. He wanted to define the form and the detail of each of these six cupolas after having built the sacristies that are covered by a differing form that of the bell towers. This would allow him to experiment with the lower cupolas in order to resolve

Finials for the fruit representing 'good deeds', decorated with Venetian mosaic.

Glass-fibre moulds composed of hyperbolic paraboloids that form the ceiling vaults for the level above the central nave. The reinforcement follows the generatrices.

The Essential Gaudí

with confidence the technical challenges the great height of the principal ones would surely present. These forms are the outcome of coupling spindles into hyperbolic paraboloids which cross their generatrices, leaving a mesh of harmoniously-organised triangles. Gaudí also planned to build a sacristy as soon as the Nativity Façade was finished. However, the start of the Civil War made it impossible to even begin this work, planned for 1936. Gaudí talked about the cupolas frequently, which is why his ideas and commentaries are conserved today. The Colonia Güell served to prove the effectiveness of vaults of double curvature supported by inclined columns.

"This project was preliminary experiment in the new architecture, and the upper level chapel was to have provided a monumental model for the nave and cupolas of the Expiatory Church, which is why it grieves me so that they did not let me leave it finished." (28)

He further stated that:

"The cupolas are the exaltation of the church. They have both exterior and interior life and throw light onto the altar, bearing in mind that the crossing is the darkest place in the church, above which there has to be the crowning element for the building, emphasising its pyramidal form." (29)

Finally, Gaudí said that:

View of the naves.

"The cupola perforated from top to bottom has no purpose, as you have to raise your eyes to see its height, losing the horizontal (which is the plane of comparison) and, as such, all sense of measurement and location." (30)

It can therefore be affirmed that these especially important elements, being the visual culmination of the church, with their pyramidal form parabolically wrapped, their figurative peaks for each assembly, have to assume the structural and plastic qualities of the sacristies. This is something that Gaudí consciously left in the hands of his successors, on the condition that they should respect his wishes by being faithful to the general ideas. It is therefore worth recording that he often spoke with his collaborators, since:

> "I know that the personal taste of the architects that follow me will influence the work, but this does not bother me. In fact, I think it will benefit the church, showing changing times within the unity of the general scheme." (31)

Even with the elements we have, it is not going to be easy to build these cupolas. For this reason, the construction of the sacristies is programmed to commence as soon as possible. This will be after all the ceiling vaults that cover the body of the church are closed so that the church can be used, in accordance with the wishes of Archbishop Cardinal of Barcelona.

The project for the sacristies has already been drawn up, the structural calculations are complete and could be built in the space of three years. From this experience, the project for the cupolas will mature and advance, just as would have occurred under Gaudí. This will be, without doubt, a huge task, due to the size of the sacristies and to the collaboration which will be required from other plastic artists, to plan with new technologies, not only for construction but also for lighting, vertical transport, acoustics, etc. Moreover, the work will have to be done at a considerable height, 100 m above the ceiling vaults with little room for manoeuvre. This is a challenge requiring courage, initiative and, above all, the will of the people, those who are really building Barcelona's new cathedral, "the church of present-day Catalonia" (32) as Gaudí liked to say.

The four bell towers for the Passion Façade, completed by the second generation of architects which succeeded Gaudí.

Puig Boada states that: "taking all problems back to their origins, botanical structure, animal movement and the geometry of mineral crystals, that is to say, the essence of Creation, are incorporated into the architecture." (33)

The Sacristies

Background and overall vision

These auxiliary buildings, which close the angles of the front giving onto Carrer de Provença, were not only destined for use as sacristies, but also for the provision of pastoral and social services and accommodation for the church custodians. They link the cloister bays that surround the church, and communicate directly with the apse, the crypt and the street. They also stem from a Gothic Revival solution passing through three levels starting from a square plan and finishing with an eight-sided cupola, with triangular pinnacles.

Between 1919 and 1920, according to Puig Boada, work continued on the new version of the sacristy, which Gaudí wished to use as the experimental model for the bell towers. The drawings were modified in accordance with the model to a point where the plan was engraved in stone. In this engraving the twelve parabolic spindles that make up the form are clearly present. Puig Boada undertook the task of reproducing all the drawings, thinking that this stone had disappeared. He drew them up again after the original was found and differences between versions were noted, though only a small discrepancy (some 30 cm in a building measuring 20 x 18 m).

The structure

The plan is inscribed in a 20 x 20 m square. Each sacristy joins three bays of cloister on each side. Gaudí planned a semi-subterranean level with openings similar to those in the rest of the cloister, already built, with inclined walls and extended openings. At the general level of the church there is space for the sacristy proper, although it is separated from the cloister. Further up there are, several more floors the possibility of subdividing the space provided by their considerable height, supported by eight inclined columns which sustain the ceiling vaults to each floor. An external staircase links the crypt

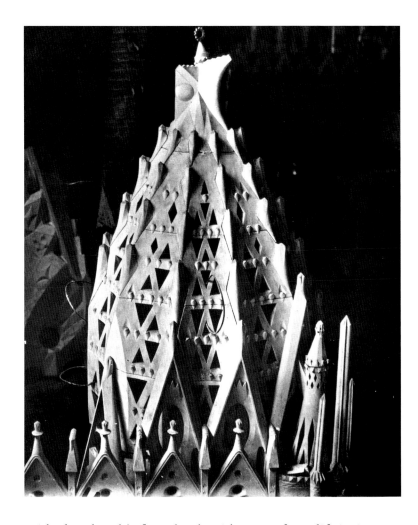

Original model for the
Sacristies made from
hyperbolic paraboloids
with the same modulation
as the rest of the church.

with the church's floor level, with space for a lift in its centre. The vaults articulate a wonderful combination of hyperboloids of revolution that gather together the mass of the columns to their collars and open at their upper part, with interlacing hyperbolic paraboloids forming a combination of octagonal stars. The lines of force coincide with the inclination of the columns. Each level is different in the way that it combines the vaults that are joined together using parabolic sections within the overall dome form of the roof. There is a large hyperbolic paraboloid with a central opening on the top level allowing the stairway to communicate with the highest part of the structure.

The roof

Gaudí planned this dome form as a singular element. It was the fruit of his deep understanding of spatial geometry and all its possibilities.

At their springing, the dozen hyperbolic paraboloid 'spindles' are unified by intersections that strengthen the assembly and provide the cupola envelope that closes the interior space. The generatrices forming each hyperbolic paraboloid in both directions are joined together by horizontal ties forming a triangular weft with proportions linked with other parts of the building: the unit, two thirds, and half in a series defined by a 15/35 m module. The pinnacles terminate the edges at four different heights reducing in volume step by step.

Architects at the Sant Cugat del Vallès School of Architecture were able to work with the original published material and the surviving models to draw the whole assembly in complete detail. Margarit and Buixadé calculated the structure required to conform with current regulations. The loads were perfectly assimilated within the dimensions Gaudí had established more than eighty years earlier.

The construction components, as Gaudí envisaged, will be prefabricated from concrete in the same way as the columns. The vaults like the side aisles, which are already finished, will be built from in situ shutters. The covering of the exterior visible surfaces and the pinnacles will be made from stone with decoration using Venetian glass.

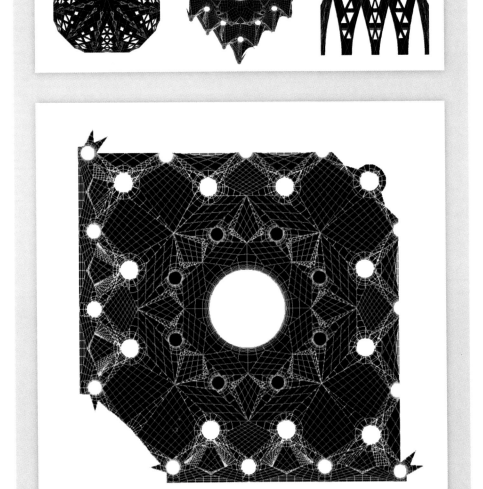

CAD drawing of the plan, elevation and perspective of the Sacristy.

General modulation

The research

Once the path that Gaudí had followed was uncovered, providing explanations for the different figures for the knots —whether they were geometrical or abstract sculptures— I found myself one day wondering about the fundamental measurements of the church, and was surprised to find that the modularity of whole, two thirds and half within the ellipsoids coincided with the 90, 60 and 45 m that are the measurements for the length of the narthex to the apse, the width of the transept and the width of the nave respectively. These measurements also coincide with the same proportions in the cross section: the vaults beneath the crossing are 60 m high, those beneath the central nave are 45 m, and those below the side aisle are 30 m.

Furthermore, the diameter of the columns keep the same relationship: the four great columns beneath the crossing have a diameter of 2.10 m, which is double the smallest which support the choir and side aisle at 1.05 m, and those of the central nave at 1.40 m, that is to say, two thirds of 2.10 m. This same relationship continues in the cross section of the side aisle at 30 m in height (the unit), the 20 m to the higher part of the terraced choir (two thirds), and 15 m to the lower part of the choir (one half). The diameters of the collars of the hyperboloids in the vaults also have the same proportions of 120, 80 and 60 cm. The intermediate columns for the side aisle, which have a diameter of 1.05 m at the lower part, and 52.5 cm higher up, and 1.575 cm for the rectangle from which they originate and provides the base for the four columns reaching up to the vaults. The macles of the pentagon and square each have 52.5 cm sides inscribed within circumferences of 52.5 and 70 cm diameter respectively, and lead to the 105 cm diameter of the circumference of the macle. Yet again the same proportions emerge: the whole, two thirds and the half.

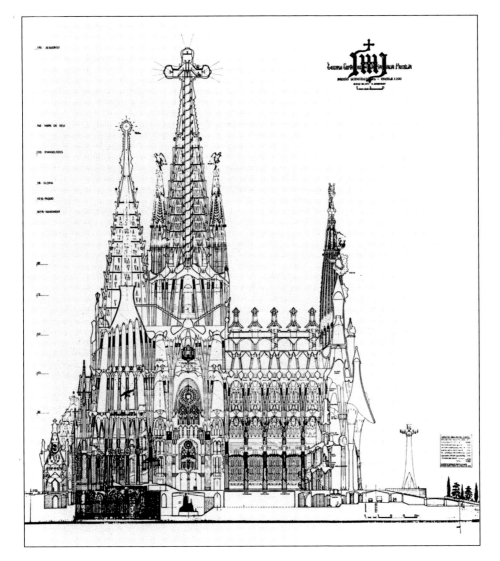

Longitudinal section
through the church.

This can also be seen with the windows: the principal ellipse has a major axis which measures 4 m, while that of the side aisle has 3 m, double that of the minor axes (2 and 1.5 m respectively). The same occurs between the minor axis of the ellipse and the circular occuli, which have dimensions of half this, and in the two in the central nave. The same is also true of those of the façade.

The Essential Gaudí

Research into a new order

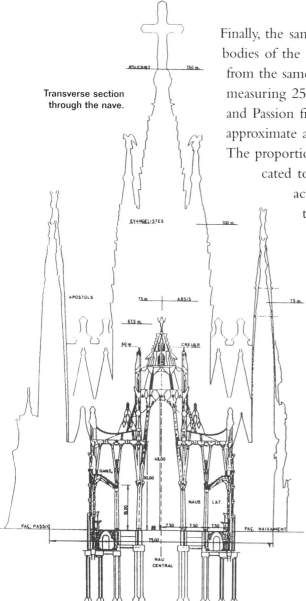

Transverse section
through the nave.

Finally, the same proportions exist between the heights for the bodies of the bell towers and the cupolas. They are all formed from the same principal element with a spire as a termination, measuring 25 m in height. The central bodies of the Nativity and Passion front bell towers are of different heights, but they approximate at 75 m with a resulting overall height of 100 m. The proportions between them are the same: the cupola dedicated to Jesus Christ reaches 150 m, 170 m taking into account the central cross. The proportions between them are also the same: the Jesus Christ Cupola 150 m (1), that of the Evangelists 100 m (2/3), and the Apostles' bell tower 75 m (1/2).

The volume in the models of the Glory Façade were also studied, showing that the different bodies that crown the hyperboloids of revolution maintain in height and diameter the same proportions described –whole, two thirds, half. Needless to say, moreover, the same proportions are found in the diameters of the corresponding spires in the form of hyperboloids of revolution which are closed by cones of the same proportions.

In completing these tasks, Gaudí brought to bear long experience gained from all his works. The Sagrada Família Church was the place where his each and every achievement should show itself in all its solidity and splendour. This was an undertaking in which improvements were made gradually and the progress made was in perfect harmony with the master's earlier work.

In his book *Gaudí, l'home i l'obra*, Bergós wrote that the measurements of all the elements of the church "form a harmonic scale of simple proportions, based on a module of 5 m but with some exceptions due to the artistic requirements of the exterior." (34)

This opinion is probably valid in part, but the results of the in-depth study demanded by having to build the church has meant that much more is now known about the proportions than was known previously. There is a proportional system that encompasses the whole building.

Model of the Glory Façade. Original study by Gaudí.

Martinell wrote: "intuition is the sculptor's domain, geometry the architect's."

Series and proportions

Professor Claudi Alsina –great grandson of one of Gaudí's collaborators, the builder of the Casa de los Botines in León– interested in the general proportions and modularity of the church, has carried out a mathematical study aimed at discovering the possible bases on which Gaudí planned the general dimensions of the Sagrada Família Church and the relations between them, taking as his starting-point comments by and conversations with the architects and collaborators in the building.

Apart from the traditional system employed over the centuries in Catalonia, based on the number twelve due to its ready divisibility by 1, 2, 3, 4, and 6, he observed that the 90 m length of the building can be divided by twelve, giving 7.5 m, which is the intercolumniation of the nave.

Thus, we have gradually related a good many of the dimensions to multiples and divisions of these figures, which have lately been confirmed as fractions: 1/4, 1/3, 1/2, 2/3, 3/4, and 1.

A number of other series also appeared which, though significant, were so due to their curiosity more than anything else. These series, however, are related to multiples and divisions of twelve, and relate both the column diameters and those of the collars of the hyperboloids of revolution or of the ellipsoids, etc. This merits illustration:

The series based on 35 and divisions thereof appear in the diameters of the columns.

210	175	140	105	70	35	17.50
6/6	5/6	4/6	3/6	2/6	1/6	1/12
1	2/3	2/3	1/2	1/3		

The heights of the towers and the cupolas are also in a series divisible by six:

150	125	100	75	50	25
6/6	5/6	4/6	3/6	2/6	1/6

Bell towers dedicated to Saint Simon and Saint Barnabas. Gaudí used reinforced concrete for the finials in 1925.

The Essential Gaudí

Research into a new order

In the measurements of width, longitude and height of the nave, the base number is fifteen and follows with its dividers:

90	75	60	45	30	15	7.5	3.75	1.875
Length of naves	Height of vaults apse	Height of vaults crossing and width of transept	Height of central nave and width of nave	Height of sides aisles and width of transept	Intermediate columns nave height of choir and width of central nave	Inter. columns nave	Inter. columns apse	Height of capital choir

Application to the arboreal structure

The distribution of dimensions for the whole of the church and above all for the arboreal structure requires modularity. Firstly, there is a general bay in the three dimensions in plane, longitudinal and transverse section. Next the dimensions of the columns and vaults are equally well linked one to another.

–Plan: the following dimensions are well-known: length, 90 m; transept, 60 m by 30 m of the total width; central nave, 45 m for the central nave; apse, 22.5 m; and nave 37.5 m.

–Transverse section: heights: choir, 15 m; side aisle vaults, 30 m; central nave, 45 m.

–The height of the longitudinal section: 45 m- the central nave; 60 m- the crossing, 75 m- the centre of the collar for the apse hyperboloid of revolution.

For the lateral vaults the height is 30 m and there is a different composition from the façade aisles as they have tiers of seats in the choirs where they flank the central nave.

These proportions are broadly reflected on page 126.

The complexity of different forms and elements from the apse to the Glory Façade mean that it is not possible to provide a complete and coherent

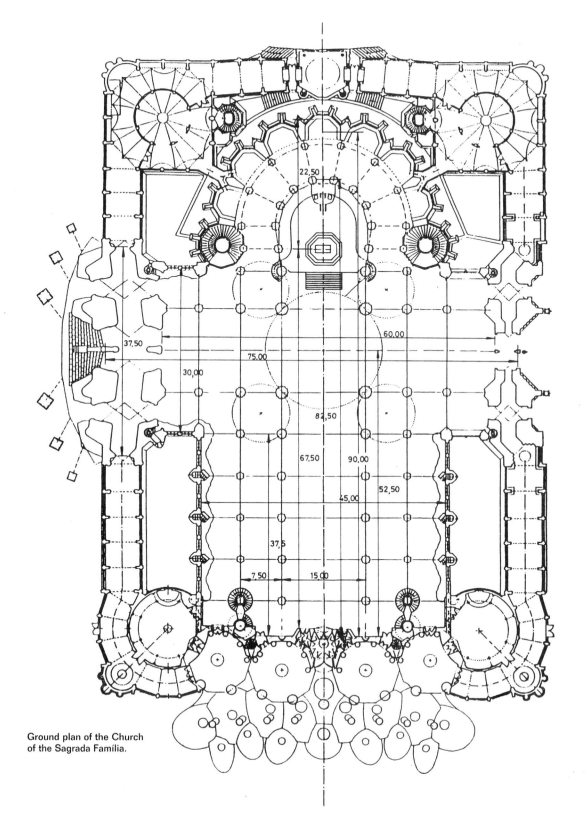

Ground plan of the Church
of the Sagrada Família.

The Essential Gaudí

Research into a new order

explanation of all the details of the Sagrada Família Church at this stage. This is a long task requiring preparation, effort and continuous dedication. The relevant models have still to be restored, a task being carried out as required by the work and when economically feasible.

	1	2	3	4	5	6	7	8	9	10	11	12
	12	11	10	9	8	7	6	5	4	3	2	1
	LENGTH	APSE ENTRANCE	PORTAL NATIVITY PASSION	TRIUMPHAL ARCH ENTRANCE	TRANSEPT	CROSSING ENTRANCE	WIDTH NAVE AND AISLES	LENGTH NAVE	CROSSING	APSE	CENTRAL NAVE	SIDE AISLE
AXES	90	82.5	75	67.5	60	52.5	45	37.5	30	22.5	15	7.5
	12/12	11/12	10/12	9/12	8/12	7/12	6/12	5/12	4/12	3/12	2/12	1/12
	6/6		5/6		4/6		3/6		2/6		1/6	
	4/4			3/4			2/4			1/4		
	3/3				2/3				1/3			
	2/2						1/2					
	210	192.5	175	157.5	140	122.5	105	87.5	70	52.5	35	17.5
COLUMNS	Dodeca-hedron		Deca-hedron		Octagon		Hexagon		Pentagon	Square	Cloister	Cloister
	3		2		2		2		1	1	1	
HYPERBOLID WINDOWS	180	165	150	135	120	105	90	75	60	45	30	15
HEIGHT OF VAULTS			75 apse		60 crossing		45 central nave		30 side aisle		15 choir	7.5 cloister

Recent findings

In July 1997, a photograph was found in the Sugrañes Archives thanks to the research of Josep Gómez Serrano and Ramon Espel. This photograph confirms that Gaudí's reasoned design process logically leads to positive results. The photograph of the 1:25 scale model shows the transept and the central nave facing

Photograph of the 1:25 scaled model for the east transept (Sugrañes Archive). This photograph confirms various hypotheses.

the Nativity Façade. This model occupies part of the space where models were on show to visitors to the church and was the result of the applications previously studied at a scale of 1:10. By keeping the scale as small as possible it was possible to show the future of more of the church as a single model. It was not possible, however, to show the full height of the bell towers in this way. The problem the interior part of the Nativity Façade presented regarding the introduction of geometrical forms of double curvature into the architecture, resolved in Gothic Revival style, must have concerned Gaudí somewhat. It is no surprise that he studied this solution using the 1:25 scale model. The photograph shows that the solution for the crossing had been studied and coincides with the work today.

Fragments of the model had been found as proof, but the photograph above provides definitive evidence. It also confirms the placing of the basalt eight sided columns at forty-five degrees to the transept and the elevation of the columns, like branches, that reach up to the vaults at 45 m. It also confirms the use of knots of lesser volume, that is, the second of the solutions known fully to us thanks to the original 1:10 scale models.

At the meeting of the transept with the façade, this photograph clearly shows the omission even of the beginnings of the ribs that take the form of tears that exist, locating the columns, which rise from behind the sculptures crowning the triforium.

The clear, neat solution Gaudí would have applied, doubtless eliminating the part already built, poses the problem of whether it is necessary to maintain all that has been done if we are to respect completely the work undertaken directly under Gaudí's supervision. It is possible that this decision will have to be taken, though before any original work is interfered with, very careful study will be required.

This discovery has at least permitted the exact location of fragments of 1:25 scale model to be worked out. Furthermore, they confirm that the 1:25 scale models were far more advanced than previously thought. The moulds exist for the balconies to the triforium and a good proportion of the angles for

View of the Nativity
Façade.

the fenestrated walls with their connections to each other. This is true both of the lower level and the elevation of the vaults, and has allowed the completion of the missing part.

Finally, on 11 August 1998, Sugrañes found, amongst the manuscripts in the archives in Capellades, part of what he had written in 1938 out of a feeling of duty to document all he knew about Gaudí, as he had had the privilege of frequenting his company so much. A phrase or two sufficed to confirm that which little by little has been discovered. To plan the church, Gaudí had made use of simple "modulated geometry," just as Bergós had claimed, and which this study aims to make more widely known.

Sugrañes wrote complaining of the destruction of the graphic information and the models, which were:

> "The basis for the continuation of the work, showing the paths which had to be followed in order to bring the work to a conclusion, the thoughts of Don Antoni, if not with the force of which only he was capable, at the very least following the directions he marked out and demonstrating the methods and procedures he used in a living way". (35)

Fortunately, the salvaged models —of whose existence Sugrañes was unaware— now restored, have made it possible to retrace Gaudí's method with the modularity and proportions they demonstrate.

All this confirms that if the line of development of Gaudí's ideas about geometry and structural forms are followed rigorously, Gaudí's own solution will be attained, or one that he would, without doubt, have arrived at, if he had been able to continue developing his architectural logic.

Conclusions

This is the result of the last years in Gaudí's life, almost a third of the time he dedicated to the Church, with the advantages of all the experience accumulated and the fact that the construction process progressed little by little due to lack of resources, developing his new architecture.

There is nothing strange about the idea that Gaudí devoted so much time to defining what he wanted the Church of the Sagrada Família to be, because in that way he left sufficient elements to make it possible to complete the work according to his ideas. He also made it clear that to his own efforts must be added those of his successors. This explains his frequent visionary statement that the creative freedom of artists who succeeded him over the years was essential, despite the need to follow the general plan defining the pyramidal envelope of the assembly of bell towers and cupolas in the exterior view, clearly shown in the drawing that has been preserved, by good fortune, in the form of a photograph.

This drawing was progressively retouched with some details added, starting with the example of the definitive studies for the sacristies, but maintaining the idea of an unchangeable whole. It is consistent with the silhouettes presented to Barcelona City Council in 1916 in order to ensure that the church setting and the vision that Gaudí had for his church was fully respected.

Model in progress at 1:25 scale.

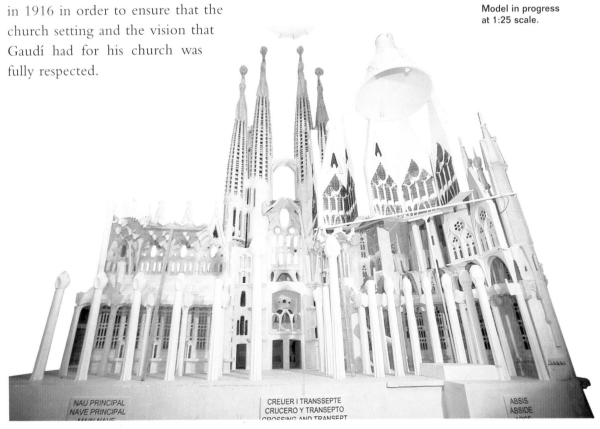

NAU PRINCIPAL
NAVE PRINCIPAL
MAIN NAVE

CREUER I TRANSSEPTE
CRUCERO Y TRANSEPTO
CROSSING AND TRANSEPT

ABSIS
ABSIDE

After Gaudí

The work after Gaudí's death

Passion Façade with
the sculptures by of
Josep Maria Subirachs.

When Gaudí died on 10 June 1926, the architect Domènec Sugrañes, as assistant, and Francesc de P. Quintana were working on the Church. The former directed the work up until the outbreak of the Spanish Civil War, the latter from the reconstruction of the crypt up until his death in 1967. All Gaudí was able to see pictured against a blue sky was the bell tower dedicated to Sant Barnaby freed of its scaffolding. The continuation of the work remained in good hands and thus in 1930, the other three bell towers in the Nativity Façade were completed, standing out in the Barcelona cityscape. The pinnacle over the central portal, with a cypress tree and various sculptures, were added to complete the iconography of the façade. The definitive stone versions of the angels singing and playing musical instruments, for which the plaster models existed, were yet to be made. The Adoration of the Kings and Shepherds, the scene of the Annunciation, for the part high above the central pointed arch and the Holy Family group located above the dividing transom of the doorway, did not yet exist and were finished little by little. The plaster models of the angel choir and musicians, which awaited their replacement by

the definitive stone versions, were smashed in 1936, later being successfully reproduced by the Japanese sculptor Etsuro Sotoo. The Holy Family group sculptures, paid for by the workers of the Bank of Bilbao, and that of the Annunciation, are the work of Jaume Busquets, whilst the kings and shepherds are by J. Ros Bofarull. They were successively installed in 1958, 1966, and 1982.

After the centenary of Gaudí's birth in 1952, the building works started up again and interest in his work began to grow. The creation of a group known as The Friends of Gaudí, presided over by Viscount Güell −Eusebi Güell i Jover− and whose dynamic secretary was Enric Casanellas, led to the organisation of the great exhibition in the Saló del Tinell in 1956. Gaudí's work was subsequently exhibited in Madrid and then Paris in 1960 at the great exhibition 'Sources of the 20th Century', accompanied by lectures, at the Museum of Modern Art. All this gradually helped to establish the figure of Gaudí in its rightful place. Until then, at an international level, Gaudí had been almost completely absent from treatises on the history of art and architecture.

The creation of the Gaudí Chair under the aegis of Josep F. Ràfols −Gaudí's first academic voice and champion− the publication of books by Cèsar Martinell, Puig Boada and Joan Bergós amongst others, and so on, sparked off the publication of a series of works and aroused growing interest all over the world. George Collins in the United States, along with J. L. Sert i Sweney, Kenji Imay in Japan, Robert Pane in Italy, etc, finishing with Joan Bassegoda, researcher and indefatigable maintainer of the Càtedra Gaudí.

The continuators

In 1957, the Sagrada Família Church Construction Committee marked the seventy fifth anniversary of the laying of the foundation stone by making a pilgrimage to Rome, where they were received by Pope Pius XII, who gave support

Domènec Sugrañes completed the cypress tree that crowns the pinnacle above the central door for the Nativity Façade.

for the continuation of the works. The vote by the Construction Committee in 1954 to build the Passion Façade and the annual collection to raise funds (known as the Capta), gave an impetus that made it possible to crown the four bell towers to the façade in 1976. The architects Puig Boada and Bonet i Garí, assisted by Joan Bergós, came to the fore at this stage, accepting the risk of executing the work from Gaudí's drawing and the challenge of the legacy with which the master had entrusted them. Particular mention should be made here, amongst other collaborators, to the architects. Dapena and Francesc de P. Cardoner, who directed the work after Bonet i Garí. It was thirty years since Gaudí's death. To the generosity of the son of a Mexican Catalan family who had visited the building as a child in his father's arms and the proceeds from the sale of some important properties which had been bequeathed to the Sagrada Família were added thousands of donations to make the work possible.

However, difficulties arose from another quarter. In 1965, a group of leading artists and intellectuals wrote an open letter to the La Vanguardia newspaper opposing the continuation of the work. This reopened a controversial issue which would continue to fan up from time to time. If Gaudí was already a controversial figure when alive, debate now centred on the possibility of continuing his great work. It was argued that, out of respect for the work of this genius, it should be left as it stood at the time of his death. Why, precisely, oppose the wishes of Gaudí, who had always wished the building to be continued? He had gone to so much trouble to provide the route, preparing plaster models of the nave, the roofs, the sacristies and a large part of the whole assembly at scales of 1:10 and 1:25 and, most importantly, he was well aware that future generations would have to finish it. He had presented the silhouette of the finished Church with the development plan for its surroundings

Manuscript written by the architect Sugrañes shortly before his death and which confirms the geometrical modulation of the church.

Gaudí completed the Nativity Façade. He wished it to embody a challenge promoting the continuation and completion of his project.

Terminals to the pinnacles with fruit (oranges) made from Venetian glass by the sculptor Etsuro Sotoo.

to Barcelona City Council early in the century, and had confirmed his project in 1916. In 1982, the centenary of the laying of the foundation stone was celebrated. Despite the recession, donations kept coming in. For this reason it is important to note the impetus given by the Archbishop of Barcelona, Narcís Jubany, in giving support to the construction of the nave in response to the popular desire that the building of the Church should continue as, year after year, his donations provided very significant economic assistance. This was a decisive intervention. Several difficult years, caused by the economic effort made to complete the bell towers for the Passion Façade with the help of bank loans, added to the economic crisis of the 1980s, meant that it was only possible to complete the finials to the apse and to commence the windows in the west nave during that decade.

At the end of the nineties, the Passion Façade, featuring Subirachs' sculptures, has finally taken on the form Gaudí's successors planned. In the blunt, naked force, well-defined and powerful, of the six inclined columns, the Passion scenes are presented with the all the crudeness required to depict the death of the crucified Christ. Moreover, the visitor entering any of the façades into the open space after so many years during which the Church interior was completely uncovered, now finds a considerable area of constructed vaults.

In late-1985, the architect Jordi Bonet was appointed to the post of Architect Director. He put together a team of architects to begin the completion of the

nave, including the professors of building structures, Drs. Joan Margarit and Carles Buixadé, who took charge of the calculations required to cover the nave.

After two years of study came the results that confirmed the viability of Gaudí's project, but which also complied with current regulations, providing for reinforcement guaranteeing the stability of the building against 200-km-hour winds at the highest parts, as well as ensuring seismic resistance. In June 1986, Josep Maria Subirachs accepted the task of creating all the sculpture for the whole Passion Façade, to be delivered within a period of 10-15 years and including around one hundred stone sculptures. Of outstanding creative capacity and the author of many outstanding works, Subirachs is now beginning to complete the whole assembly.

The foundations to the nave and half the crossing and transept took the best part of four years while, little by little, the nave fronts and windows were being

built. There are more than four kilometres of piles in total, reaching a depth of 20 m down to tertiary rock to avoid any differential settlement. The pile heads need to resist enormous loads up to eight thousand tonnes load, with the columns for the crossing being the most exacting. The construction of the Doric columns in the market-place in Parc Güell, based on prefabricated elements approximately one metre high with the decorative broken tile mosaic serving as covering for concrete or masonry, the columns also carrying the conduits for the water borne to the great underground cistern, provides the  precedent, employing the same system by which the supporting columns for the Sagrada Família Church nave and aisles were built, with corresponding reinforcement and stone from Montjuïc, granite, basalt and porphyry forming the skin. Gaudí had experimented with the use of reinforced concrete in the Parc Güell project as well as for the finials to the Nativity Façade. In the latter, the use of Portland cement has been confirmed.

He had also clearly stated, in the lecture he gave in 1923 to the Associació d'Arquitectes de Catalunya, his intention to reinforce the supporting columns in the Church and his reasons for doing so. It was therefore quite clear that this was the route to be followed.

Cèsar Martinell had noted it in his conversations with Gaudí. The very architects who continued the facultative direction of the work used to speak of 'synthetic stone', differentiating this from what, in that period, was known as 'artificial stone'.

Nowadays, the name 'architectural', or precast concrete forms part of the vocabulary of construction. It is based on prefabricated pieces with forms from

Ecce homo, a sculpture
by Josep Maria Subirachs.

moulds of diverse materials and concretes of the colour of choice with excellent strengths according to results obtained through laboratory analysis. The reinforcement increases the possible tension forces that stone is able to resist and thus contributes admirably to resisting seismic jolts or winds up to 200 kilometres per hour. The requirements of current legislation are very different from those in force seventy years ago, making necessary this reinforcement which, moreover, allows the lateral vaults as well to be built independently of those of the centre or the crossing, using lightweight scaffolding and avoiding the need to wait for the whole of Gaudí's planned arborescent structure to be in place to take any forces in complete equilibrium.

The greater resistance of steel −5100 Kg/cm²− and special concretes −up to 800 Kg/cm²− has allowed the sections to be maintained as Gaudí had planned, despite the more exacting building regulations.

La Verònica, a sculpture by Josep Maria Subirachs.

By early-1993, the first section of the vaults supporting the choir on the west side had seen the light. The event brought to mind what the Master, full of faith in his work, had said, back in the twenties, according to Lluís Bonet i Garí, the last remaining survivor of his disciples. When he was informed, just a few hours before his own death, that the light glided across those surfaces, Bonet answered: "What did you expect?"

Now the vaults above the side aisle are visible, and those for the central nave are nearing completion. Those for the transept are on the way too. The structural studies for the crossing and the apse are well advanced. Very soon those for the sacristies will be finished. These, once complete, will allow the experience to be acquired that Gaudí sought from building them, so that the definitive solution could be reached for the cupola dedicated to Jesus Christ.

One might even begin to hope that, as long as sufficient economic resources are forthcoming, it will be possible to have the vaults closed for the whole ensemble by the 150th anniversary of Gaudí's birth, on 25 June 2002.

Aided by computers, the original plaster models are beginning to be transcribed so that they can be executed with complete fidelity. The enthusiastic dedication of the team of architects led by Professor Josep Gómez Serrano –Head of Department of Structures at the Polytechnic University of Catalonia School of Architecture– is provided in the framework of a co-operation agreement with the Church Construction Committee. Also of importance is the work undertaken by the architect Professor Mark Burry, at Victoria University of Wellington (NZ) up to June 1996 and at Deakin University in Australia since, in determining the geometry of the windows and roof of the nave and aisles.

The granite and basalt columns have been cut using computer-controlled machinery thanks to the equations that derive the helicoids that generate them. Lately, a new machine has been introduced which copies them in stone at full scale from a plaster model. The pace of building has increased notably through the introduction of the new technology and the use of computers.

It is clear that much remains to be finished before the central cupola can be crowned with the Cross. There are still many unknowns that need clarification, and doubts to be resolved. Keeping faith with Gaudí's design demands rigorous efforts in research to overcome difficulties. It is not only a question of finance for this building, just about half-finished as we enter the 21st century.

Techniques, architects and other collaborators, that is, the successors Gaudí confidently predicted that Providence would provide, continue to be needed to complete the work.

Passion Façade.
The Apostle Saint Barnabas.
Sculpted by Josep Maria
Subirachs.

The Essential Gaudí

The future of Gaudí's architecture

It seems clear that Gaudí's architecture, despite being temporally located in Modernism and although much of his work can be described as Modernist, is nevertheless a singular, unrepeatable phenomenon. If it is unrepeatable, it follows that it would be more prudent not to follow in his footsteps. This would seem to be the most reasonable line to take, and is that which the majority have opted for, wrongly, in my view.

Noucentisme, a highly influential style during the last twenty years of Gaudí's life, and which invokes classicism and Mediterranean light, was also a reaction against Modernism.

Gaudí agreed in part with these premises. He stated that the Church "is Hellenic in spirit" (36) and that, "in making this church I have proposed to follow a tradition of our own, a tradition congenial to us, the Mediterranean tradition. True art has always been in the Mediterranean." (37) It is true that much of critical opinion and many Noucentistes could not agree with Gaudí, and something of a backlash against Gaudí's work was produced on the part of critics and intellectual and artistic circles. Feliu Elias, 'Apa', who had at one point eulogised his work, was now ferocious in his criticism, and this attitude became fashionable. Even Ràfols, undeniably an unflagging, faithful admirer of Gaudí's work, as well as a great friend and collaborator of Lluis Bonet Garí's, advised him not to follow the trail blazed by Gaudí. "Forget it, it will only cause you problems", said Ràfols to his friend.

Despite all, some of his collaborators followed the Master's teachings, building works that Cèsar Martinell categorised as "Gaudinian". Josep Maria Jujol and Rubió i Bellver are two cases in point. Equilibrated arches were important elements in the work of Puig i Cadafalch, Cèsar Martinell and Gaudí's more direct successors Isidre Puig Boada, Lluis Bonet i Garí and Joan Bergós, who used Gaudinian geometry in Catalonia.

The colours in the façade and bell towers symbolise life.

Milagrosa Church,
Mexico, by the architect
Felix Candela.

Ruled surfaces have been used for very different purposes, notably in the form of the hyperboloid of revolution, as were also employed in Russia in the 1920s by Suslov, who used them to locate towers and antennae for Radio Moscow. They are still there, visible at a height of over 100 m. It was not until the 1950s and 1960s, however, that great architects of international renown decided to use them. In Mexico, Félix Candela has carried out spectacular projects using hyperbolic paraboloids, whilst in Brasilia Oscar Niemeyer used a hyperboloid of revolution to generate the enclosing ribs for his new cathedral. Even Le Corbusier used ruled surfaces for the Philips Pavilion at the Brussels Exhibition in 1960. Saarinen also built the huge TWA facilities at New York airport using forms of this type. On a minor scale, I myself have been able to construct the churches of Vinyoles d'Oris and Sant Medir following this method and Gaudí's proposals. Even structural calculations have been carried out by means of hanging models.

Brasilia Cathedral, by the architect Oscar Niemeyer.

In another variant, the roofs of the buildings for the Munich Olympic Games, by Frei Otto, form an original and highly-developed continuation of Gaudí's ideas. A university professor in Stuttgart, Frei Otto was the driving-force behind a group of German and Dutch researchers who rebuilt the hanging model of the chapel at Colònia Güell with all its profusion of little bags of bird shot, cords and wire. Neglect and abandonment had, unfortunately, led to the loss of the original at Santa Coloma de Cervelló.

Reticulated structures and space, of which Gaudí made first use, are regularly applied today.

"My ideas have an indisputable logic, and the only thing that troubles me is that they have not been applied more and that I was the first to do so; it is the only thing that might cause me to doubt." (38)

The Essential Gaudí

Reproduction of the hanging model of the chapel at the Colònia Güell. The model was made by a team directed by the architectural engineer Frei Otto and such others as Jos Tomlow and Rainer Graefe.

"I first tried out the structure which will be used for the Sagrada Família Church at the Colònia Güell. Without this previous trial, I would not have dare to adopt it for the church." (39)

That which, until recently, was difficult to project, that is to say, to see in space and then reproduce in plans, calculating forces, has now become something feasible to achieve through the use of the computer. I do not believe, however, that this is something that could be seen as a valid solution for buildings destined to serve as housing or offices generally speaking. Nevertheless, I am convinced that it opens up creative paths for singular or monumental buildings. It is not a question of suggesting that Gaudí represents only the future of an architecture in stone, but one of opening up to the entire range of present and future technology capable of forming part of a composition in which light, space, rationality and use achieve spaces and volumes creating harmony and aesthetic emotion.

Aerial view of the Church of the Sagrada Família, rising majestically amidst the urban landscape (2001).

The Essential Gaudí

Saint Medir Church,
Barcelona, by the architect
Jordi Bonet.

Ruled forms in all their variants, and not just surfaces, are the great opportunity which Gaudí brings to the history of architecture, opening up a future that is only just beginning in the process of reticulated structures in space.

The long hours so many generations of architects spent drawing the classical orders or the repertory of styles over the centuries were employed, to a large extent, in the task of assimilating their proportions and the sensitivity required to achieve the capacity to propose them and make them understandable on the part of developers and consumers of architecture. The great contribution of the avant-garde and rationalist movements this century must be understood as the best solution to the economic and social problems of these new times. Their general acceptance does not require comment. But could it be a positive step to pass up the opportunity of following Gaudí's proposals?

Vistabella Church, by the architect Josep Maria Jujol.

Creativity must always be free of prejudices of style or aesthetic dictates, which often obey particular economic interests more than objective reality. In the case of Gaudí, much learning will be obtained from following in the master's footsteps but, above all, and without the shadow of a doubt, we can also achieve the freedom he defends. This is a rigorous proposal, to study each problem within the social function of architecture at the service of people and communities, in accordance with nature, which continues to be the master and fount of inspiration, where there is a spirit of observation and a deep respect for the demands relating to the uses a building can be put to and to the possibilities of materials and technique. All this presents a real opportunity for creation and progress.

Thus it is contemporary; as such, it is an open road. With the use of infinite lines in space, generators of volumes and of possibilities, Gaudí opened up a path offering a creative, fully harmonious process, a trail he blazed as the best means of providing people with beautiful shelter through architecture.

Gaudí insisted with conviction that in the work of building the Church of the Sagrada Família "We all have to contribute, because it has to be a church for a whole people", adding that:

> "This will be the church of present-day Catalonia. I remember that someone once told me that historically, Catalonia has never been anything, and I replied that if this were the case it would be a reason to believe that it must still become something and that we all have to work towards this." (40)

Gaudí created a new architecture and held a contagious faith based on his optimistic vision of the situation because "important works cannot be achieved without optimism." (41)

Let us be workers, then, so that the new architecture which Gaudí began and of which the Sagrada Família Church is the greatest exponent, shall continue to demand dedication, love, effort and optimism to carry it forward. The work richly deserves it.

Corpus Christi procession in Barcelona (1924). At the steps up to the Cathedral,
Gaudí with his colleagues from the Cercle Artístic de Sant Lluc.

Notes

(1) BERGÓS, J. *Antoni Gaudí: L'home i l'obra*, p. 56.

(2) MARTÍ MATLLEU, J. "Impresiones acerca del Templo de la Sagrada Família".

(3) MARTINELL, C. *Gaudí i la Sagrada Família comentada per ell mateix*, 102, quoted in PUIG BOADA, I. *El pensament de Gaudí*, p. 102.

(4) *El Propagador de la Devoción de San José*, March 1902.

(5) MARTINELL, C. *Ob. cit.*, p. 43, in PUIG BOADA, I. *Ob. cit.*, p. 193.

(6) SUGRAÑES, D. "Disposició estàtica del Temple de la Sagrada Família", p. 17-36.

(7) MARTINELL, C. *Ob. cit.*, p. 125.

(8) MATAMALA, J. *Mi itinerario con el arquitecto*, p. 580 i 583.

(9) PUIG BOADA, I. *El Temple de la Sagrada Família*, 1929.

(10) PUIG BOADA, I. *El pensament* [...], p. 108.

(11) BERGÓS, J. *Conversaciones de Gaudí y Juan Bergós*, p. 174, quoted in PUIG BOADA, I. *El pensament* [...], p. 153.

(12) BERGÓS, J. *Gaudí, el hombre y la obra*, p. 57, quoted in PUIG BOADA, I. *El pensament* [...], p. 213.

(13) BERGÓS, J. *Gaudí, el hombre* [...], p. 37, quoted in PUIG BOADA, I. *El pensament* [...], p. 171.

(14) ARGIMON, J. "Com es va salvar de ser volat el Temple".

(15) PUIG BOADA, I. *El Temple de* [...].

(16) BERGÓS, J. *Gaudí, el hombre* [...], p. 389, quoted in PUIG BOADA, I. *El pensament* [...], p. 98.

(17) BERGÓS, J. *Conversaciones de* [...], p. 217, quoted in PUIG BOADA, I. *El pensament* [...], p. 93.

(18) BERGÓS, J. *Conversaciones de* [...], p. 123, quoted in PUIG BOADA, I. *El pensament* [...], p. 93.

(19) MARTINELL, C. *Ob. cit.*, p. 87, quoted in PUIG BOADA, I. *El pensament* [...], p. 99.

(20) BERGÓS, J. *Conversaciones de* [...], p. 101, quoted in PUIG BOADA, I. *El pensament* [...], p. 92-93.

(21) MARTINELL, C. *Ob. cit.*, p. 86, quoted in PUIG BOADA, I. *El pensament* [...], p. 99.

(22) BERGÓS, J. *Conversaciones de* [...], p. 175, quoted in PUIG BOADA, I. *El pensament* [...], p. 208.

(23) BERGÓS, J. *Conversaciones de* [...], p. 161, quoted in PUIG BOADA, I. *El pensament* [...], p. 208.

(24) BERGÓS, J. *Gaudí, el hombre* [...], p. 57, quoted in PUIG BOADA, I. *El pensament* [...], p. 213.

(25) MARTINELL, C. *Ob. cit.*, p. 125, quoted in PUIG BOADA, I. *El pensament* [...], p. 207.

(26) SUGRAÑES, D. *Ob. cit.*, p. 17-36.

(27) MARTINELL, C. *Ob. cit.*, p. 78, quoted in PUIG BOADA, I. *El pensament* [...], p. 210.

(28) BERGÓS, J. *Gaudí, el hombre* [...], p. 102, quoted in PUIG BOADA, I. *El pensament* [...], p. 207.

(29) BONET, J. *Temple Sagrada Família*.

(30) BERGÓS, J. *Conversaciones de* [...], p. 57, quoted in PUIG BOADA, I. *El pensament* [...], p. 118.

(31) MARTINELL, C. *Ob. cit.*, p. 43, quoted in PUIG BOADA, I. *El pensament* [...], p. 193.

(32) MARTINELL, C. *Ob. cit.*, p. 39, quoted in PUIG BOADA, I. *El pensament* [...], p. 196.

(33) PUIG BOADA, I. *El Temple de la Sagrada Família*, p. 122.

(34) BERGÓS, J. *Gaudí, l'home i l'obra*, p. 149.

(35) "Sugrañes Manuscript" in the archives of the Col·legi d'Arquitectes de Catalunya.

(36) BASSEGODA, J. *El Gran Gaudí*.

(37) PUIG BOADA, I. *El Templo de* [...].

(38) PUIG BOADA, I. *El Temple de* [...], p. 180.

(39) MARTINELL, C. *Ob. cit.*, p. 87, quoted in PUIG BOADA, I. *El pensament* [...], p. 99.

(40) MARTINELL, C. *Ob. cit.*, p. 39, quoted in PUIG BOADA, I. *El pensament* [...], p. 196.

(41) MARTINELL, C. *Ob. cit.*, p. 113, quoted in PUIG BOADA, I. *El pensament* [...], p. 193.

Bibliography

Àlbum del Temple Expiatori de la Sagrada Família. Asociación Espiritual de Devotos de San José, Barcelona, 1917, 1920, 1926.

Àlbum Record a Gaudí i al Temple Expiatori de la Sagrada Família. Barcelona, 1936.

ARGIMON, J. "Com es va salvar de ser volat el Temple". *Temple*, 131, p. 19 (1997).

ARTIGAS AMAT, R. "Gaudí creador d'estructures". *La Veu de Catalunya* (11-VI-1928).

BASSEGODA, J. *Gaudí, vida i arquitectura.* Barcelona, 1977, p. 206-207.
  – *La arquitectura de Gaudí.* Editorial Planeta, Barcelona, 1982.
  – *Gaudí. La arquitectura del futuro.* "la Caixa"/ Salvat Editores, Barcelona, 1984.
  – *El Gran Gaudí.* Editorial Ausa, Sabadell, 1989.
  – *Antoni Gaudí.* Edicions 62 / Península, Barcelona, 1992.
  – L'Estudi de Gaudí: selecció d'articles publicats a la revista *Temple entre 1971 i 1994.* Temple Expiatori de la Sagrada Família, 1996.

BENET, R. "Fent coneixença amb Le Corbusier". *La Veu de Catalunya* (21-V-28).

BERGÓS, J. *Gaudí, l'home i l'obra.* Editorial Ariel, Barcelona, 1954.
  – *"Las conversaciones de Gaudí con Juan Bergós".* Hogar y arquitectura (May-June 1974), Madrid.
  – *Gaudí, el hombre y la obra.* Universitat Politècnica de Catalunya, Barcelona, 1974.
  – *Tabicados huecos.* Col·legi Ofical d'Arquitectes de Catalunya, Barcelona, 1965.

BONET, J. *El Temple de la Sagrada Família.* Escudo de Oro, Barcelona, 1992.
  – *Gaudí. Dibuixos originals. Originals drawings.* Junta Constructora del Temple Expiatori de la Sagrada Família, Barcelona, 1996.
  – *Temple Sagrada Família.* Escudo de Oro, Barcelona, 1997.

BURRY, M.C. *The Expiatory Church of the Sagrada Família.* Phaidon, London, 1993.

CARDELLACH, F. "Explicació de Gaudí sobre les voltes de paraboloides, i estructura arborífera". *El Propagador*, 14, year IL (15-VII-1915).

CASANELLAS, R. *Nueva visión de Gaudí.* Editorial Polígrafa, Barcelona, 1965.

CIRICI PELLICER, A. *La Sagrada Família de Antonio Gaudí.* Ediciones Omega, Barcelona, 1952.

CIRLOT, J.E. *El arte de Gaudí.* Ediciones Omega, Barcelona, 1965 (3rd edition).

COLLINS, G.R. *Antoni Gaudí.* Braziller, New York, 1960.

"El somni realitzat". *La Veu de Catalunya*, 2437 (20-I-1906).

FLORES, C. *Gaudí, Jujol y el Modernismo catalán.* Aguilar, Madrid, 1983.

GÓMEZ SERRANO, J. *L'obrador de Gaudí.* Edicions UPC, Barcelona, 1996.

GÓMEZ SERRANO, J., COLL, J., MELERO, J. i BURRY, M. *La Sagrada Família: de Gaudí al CAD.* Edicions UPC, Barcelona, 1996.

JOHNSON SWEENEY, J. i SERT, J.L. *Antoni Gaudí.* Ediciones Infinito, Buenos Aires, 1960.

Jornadas Internacionales de Estudios Gaudinistas. Col·legi Oficial d'Arquitectes de Catalunya, Ediciones Blume, Barcelona, 1970.

LAHUERTA, J.J. *Antoni Gaudí 1885-1926. Arquitectura, ideología y política.* Electa España, Madrid, 1993.

LE CORBUSIER. *Gaudí.* Editorial RM, Barcelona, 1958.
  – *"Antonio Gaudí: estructura y forma".* Dins: S. TARRAGÓ, *Antoni Gaudí.* Ediciones del Serbal, Barcelona, 1991, pp. 109-130.

"Manifestació de Gaudí de no treballar més que al Temple de la Sagrada Família". *Diario de Barcelona* (24-XII-1914).

MARTÍ MATLLEU, J. "Impresiones acerca del Templo de la Sagrada Família". *Diari de Barcelona*

(6-III-14, 10-III-14, 19-III-14, 27-III-14, 4-IV-14, 5-V-14, 15-V-14).

MARTINELL, C. *Gaudí i la Sagrada Família comentada per ell mateix.* Aymà, S. L. Editores, Barcelona, 1951.

– *Gaudinismo.* Publicaciones Amigos de Gaudí, Barcelona, 1954.

– *Gaudí, su vida, su teoría, su obra.* Col·legi Oficial d'Arquitectes de Catalunya i Balears, Barcelona, 1967.

– *Conversaciones con Gaudí.* Editorial Punto Fijo, Barcelona, 1969.

MATAMALA, J. *Mi itinerario con el arquitecto.* Unpublished, Barcelona, 1965.

PERUCHO, J. *Gaudí, una arquitectura de anticipación.* Ediciones Polígrafa, Barcelona, 1967.

PLA, J. *Homenots.* Editorial Destino, Barcelona, 1969, vol. I.

POBLET, J.M. *Gaudí, l'home i el geni.* Editorial Bruguera, Barcelona, 1973.

PRÉVOST, C. i DESCHARNES, R. *La visió artística i religiosa de Gaudí.* Aymà, Barcelona, 1969.

PUIG BOADA, I. *El Temple de la Sagrada Família.* Editorial Barcino, Barcelona,1929.

– *El Templo de la Sagrada Família.* Ediciones Omega, 2nd edition,Barcelona, 1952.

– *El pensament de Gaudí*, Col·legi d'Arquitectes de Catalunya i Balears, Barcelona, 1981.

– *El Temple de la Sagrada Família.* Nuevo Arte Thor, 4rh edition, Barcelona, 1982.

PUJOLS, F. *La visió artística i religiosa d'en Gaudí.* Barcelona, 1927.

QUINTANA, F. de P. "Les formes guerxes del Temple de la Sagrada Família". *La Ciutat i la Casa*, 6 (1927), p. 16-29.

RÀFOLS, J.F. *Antonio Gaudí.* Ed. Canosa, 2nd edition, Barcelona, 1929.

– *Gaudí, 1852-1926.* Editorial Aedos, 3rd edition, Barcelona, 1952.

RÀFOLS, J.F. i FOLGUERA, F. *Gaudí.* Ed. Canosa, Barcelona, 1928.

SOLÀ-MORALES, I. *Gaudí.* Ediciones Polígrafa, Barcelona, 1984.

"Solució definitiva de les voltes d'hiperboloides. Fases principals (maqueta) del projecte definitiu de les sagristies". *El Propagador*, year LVI, 7, (1-IV-1922), pp. 103-104.

SUGRAÑES, D. "Disposició estàtica del Temple de la Sagrada Família". *Anuari Associació d'Arquitectes de Catalunya*, Barcelona, 1923, pp. 17-36.

– "Explicación del gravado de la sección longitudinal del Templo". *El Propagador*, 9, year LI (1-V-1917), pp. 148-153.

– "Informe de las obras". *El Propagador*, 14, year LIV (5-VII-1920), pp. 215-258.

– "Se va a terminar un campanario". *El Propagador*, 1, year LIX (1-I-1925), p. 22.

"Suplement: homenatge a Antoni Gaudí". *El Matí*, Barcelona (21-VI-36).

TARRAGÓ, S. *Gaudí.* Escudo de Oro, Barcelona, 1974.

TORII, T. *El mundo enigmático de Gaudí.* Instituto de España-Madrid, Madrid, 1983.

VINCI, L. *Antoni Gaudí.* Ediciones Nauta, Barcelona, 1970.

Photographers

Salvador Redó: p. 35, 36, 39, 39, 41, 49, 50, 52 sup., 53, 55, 59, 66, 70, 76, 82, 83, 85, 86, 87, 91, 93, 94, 95, 96, 98, 99, 102, 104, 109 sup., 123, 129, 131, 133, 135, 138, 139, 140, 141, 142, 143, 145, 147

Jordi Bonet: p. 12, 19, 25, 44, 52 inf., 57, 61, 64, 72, 80, 89, 109 inf., 111, 148, 149, 152

Jordi Faulí: p. 105

Arxiu del Temple Expiatori de la Sagrada Família: p. 15, 17, 19 sup., 20, 23, 24, 26, 27, 29, 30, 31, 33, 43, 45, 47, 51, 107, 115, 119, 121, 127, 130, 151, 155

Joaquim Camp: p. 76, 85, 99

TAVISA: p. 150

ECSA: p. 11, 150, 137